D0866061

FOR REFERENCE ONLY

G1 CPPR

www.lancashire.gov.uk/libraries

1349   LL2(A)

Tracing your Nineteenth Century Family History

Stuart A. Raymond

FAMILY HISTORY CENTURY BY CENTURY

Published by:
Federation of Family History Societies
(Publications) Ltd.,
Units 15-16, Chesham Industrial Estate,
Oram Street, Bury,
Lancashire BL9 6EN

in association with:
S.A. & M.J.Raymond
P.O.Box 35, Exeter EX1 3YZ
Email: samjraymond@btopenworld.com
Http: www.samjraymond.btinternet.co.uk/igb.htm

ISBNs:
Federation of Family History Societies: 1-86006-186-9
S.A. & M.J. Raymond: 1-899668-40-3

Printed and bound by the Alden Group, Oxford OX2 0EF

Contents

Introduction

It is probably easier to research family history in the nineteenth century, or, at least, in the period from 1837, than for any other long period. This is due to the fact that the researcher has available two major comprehensive sources - the records of civil registration from 1837, and the census enumerators' schedules every ten years from 1841. These two sources should, in theory, enable the genealogist to trace the bare bones of his family tree without recourse to other sources. In practice, however, both sources are liable to human error, and if information cannot be found in them it must be sought in the multitude of other sources that are available. The latter must also be consulted if the researcher wants to do more than merely construct a pedigree.

The purpose of this book is to encourage you to do just that, to go beyond the bare bones of the civil registers and census, and to understand the history of your family in its social and economic setting - how they lived and worked, their triumphs and failures, their religion and politics, their place in society. Family history should be more than the bare bones of pedigrees.

Nineteenth century records offer the family historian an enormous amount of information. If information from civil registration and census records can be combined with details from electoral registers and poll books, trade directories, occupational sources, poor law and parish records, and the wide variety of other sources available, much can be discovered. The sources discussed in this book are simply the ones which are best known and most accessible. There are many others to be found in libraries, record offices, in family homes, and elsewhere.

This book is intended as a basic introduction to sources which are readily accessible. I have tried to identify web pages and books that provide more detailed guidance where they exist; mostly, full details are given at the end of each chapter. Internet addresses are liable to rapid change, and the URLs listed here may be different by the time you read this book; however, if you search the titles of sites on a search engine such as Google (**www.google.com**), you should be able to locate those which have moved addresses,

This book is the second volume of a series which will describe, century by century, the records available to genealogists. *Tracing your twentieth century family history* has already been published; a small amount of information common to both periods is repeated here from that volume, and in particular chapters 1 & 2 - which provide vital information for all researchers - may be skipped if you have read the twentieth century volume.

As we proceed to draw up our family trees, we need

to know where we would be likely to find information on our ancestors at particular dates. The purpose of this book will have been achieved if it enables you to identify a variety of different sources all throwing light on your family history in the nineteenth century.

In writing this book, I have relied heavily on the books and web pages listed at the end of this introduction. On most subjects, I have checked what Herber, Hey and Fitzhugh have written. The holdings of the National Archives are described in detail on its web site, and also by Bevan. Anyone writing on genealogical sources is obliged to sit on the shoulders of giants, and we must all be grateful for the work of authors such as these. This book has been typed by Cynthia Hanson, and seen through the press by Bob Boyd. My thanks to them, to Exeter University Library, where much of my research has been done, and to my family for their support.

Web Page
- National Archives
  www.nationalarchives.gov.uk

Further Reading
- HERBER, MARK D. *Ancestral trails: the complete guide to British genealogy and family history.* 2nd ed. Stroud: Sutton Publishing / London: Society of Genealogists, 2004.
- HEY, DAVID. *The Oxford companion to local and family history.* Oxford University Press, 1996.

- FITZHUGH, TERRICK V.H. *The dictionary of genealogy.* 5th ed., revised by Susan Lumas. A & C Black, 1998.
- RAYMOND, STUART A. *Family history: a pocket dictionary.* F.F.H.S., 2003.
- BEVAN, AMANDA. *Tracing your ancestors in the Public Record Office.* 6th ed. Public Record Office 19. P.R.O., 2002.

Chapter 1

Sources of Information:
the Internet, Books, Libraries, Record
Offices, Family History Societies

Information about your family history may be found in
a wide variety of places - amongst old papers in your
home (or in the homes of relatives), in graveyards, in the
records to be found in church safes, *etc.* But most
written sources are likely to be found in libraries and
record offices. The internet provides a great deal of
information for nineteenth century researchers, and is
likely to be the first port of call for genealogists, if only
because it is available in most homes and is so quick
and easy to access. That does have its drawbacks.
Accuracy and comprehensiveness on web pages are not
always all that they should be; with a few exceptions,
they should not be regarded as authoritative, but should
always be viewed critically. A detailed introduction to
internet resources is provided by Christian, and no
attempt will be made here to replicate his work. The
present author's *Family History on the Web* provides a
directory of the most important web sites, and is
complemented by the other volumes in his *F.F.H.S. web
directories* series: these are intended to be used as you
would use a telephone directory.

A vast number of web pages for genealogists are currently available; by the time you read this there will be many more. They offer:

- advice
- details of organisations such as family history societies, record offices and libraries (including many library catalogues)
- interests lists and mailing lists which enable you to make contact with others researching the same surname.
- databases, transcripts and indexes of original sources.
- historical and genealogical information relating to particular families.

The advice offered on the web is usually fairly basic, and genealogical textbooks often provide much more information. The prime exception to this rule are the many 'research guides' on the National Archives site (click on 'getting started'), which are authoritative on particular sources. Before visiting libraries, record offices, and societies you should always check their web-sites, which usually provide the most up-to-date information concerning their opening hours, holdings, and activities. Web-based interests lists, and sites for particular families, are normally unique to the internet. A wide variety of original sources have been transcribed and/or indexed on web pages; there are a sufficient number of baptism, marriage and death registers, monumental inscriptions, and war memorials, for each of these categories to be the subject of a volume or two in the present author's *F.F.H.S. web directories* series. Most of these pages are relatively small; however, a significant number of sizeable pages are provided by *Family History Online*, which hosts databases compiled by family history societies, including a number relating to the nineteenth century.

The best on-line guide to web resources for British genealogy is the extensive *Genuki* site, which is the subject of Hawgood's useful guide book. The site provides over 20,000 pages of advice and information, including many transcripts and indexes of original sources. *Genuki* is complemented by *Cyndis List*, which is an extensive online directory of web-sites (also available in book format). *Cyndi's List* is international in scope, with far more North American content than British, but nevertheless should be consulted by all genealogists seeking web-sites on particular subjects.

Books (with CD's and microfiche) offer genealogists far more information then the internet, and in some cases, e.g. the Parliamentary papers, (see chapter 18) and trade directories (see chapter 13) are themselves primary sources of information; many of them have been reproduced on CD or microfiche. Numerous other primary sources have been transcribed and/or indexed for publication; for example, much of the census is now available on CD, and numerous census indexes have been published by family history societies as booklets or microfiche. Many thousand books on nineteenth century history have been published; those of direct relevance to the family historian may be identified by consulting the various volumes of Raymond's *British genealogical library guides* series. The study of family history does require an understanding of the wider historical background, and it may be found useful to dip into the authoritative bibliographies of British history by Brown and Christie, and by Hanham, in order to identify those books which are most likely to aid understanding on particular topics. Bibliographies are important: they should be one of the first ports of call for any enquiry, since they will tell you where to find the published information you need.

Once you have identified the books that you need to consult, you will want to obtain copies of them. It may be worth purchasing those you are likely to consult repeatedly, such as bibliographies and handbooks. Any bookshop should be able to supply books which are in print. The publications of family history societies, as listed by Perkins (for microfiche) and Hampson (for books) are best purchased direct from publishers, or via *GENfair* (**www.genfair.com**) on the internet. Out of print books may be more difficult to obtain. Many have been reprinted on CD, and can be identified by consulting Raymond's *British family history on CD,* or by checking the web-sites of CD publishers. There are also many sites on the internet which enable you to search the stock of hundreds of second-hand booksellers. You may be able to make contact via the web with someone able to look up a particular reference for you: a number of web-sites are devoted to look-ups. Virtually all published books are available in libraries, and most (unless they are rare) may be borrowed, usually at a small cost, via inter-library loan through most public libraries.

Libraries are warehouses of books, periodicals and microfiche, and sometimes hold manuscript materials. A detailed discussion of their uses is provided by Raymond's *Using libraries*. Local studies libraries may be particularly useful, since they generally aim to maintain a comprehensive collection of everything published concerning the area they cover, and are able to offer specialist advice. The general reference sections of public libraries may also be useful; they usually have genealogical collections, and may hold published source material for many parts of the country. London's Guildhall Library, for example, holds the publications and journals of many family history societies, and has one of the most extensive collections of trade directories in the country.

Good collections of nineteenth-century British history are also frequently held by university libraries, especially those which support a history department. Although their collection policies rarely have the genealogist in mind, nevertheless they do hold a great deal of information; for example, a noteworthy collection of poll books is held by the Institute of Historical Research, and the University of

Leicester is making its extensive collection of trade directories available via the internet.

The libraries and resources of family history societies are also important. They have created and hold innumerable indexes and transcripts of source material, which have sometimes also been deposited with both the local studies library and the Society of Genealogists. An increasing number of their indexes are available on the Family History Online website. Many transcripts and indexes have been published, and are listed in both the county volumes of Raymond's *British genealogical library guides* series, and in the listings of Perkins and Hampson. The Society of Genealogists probably has the largest family history library in the United Kingdom, rivalled only by the British Library. The resoures of the largest genealogical library in the world - the Family History Library in Salt Lake City, run by the Latter Day Saints, can be tapped into from any of their Family History Centres, which can be found in most major cities throughout the world. Its website, *Family Search*, provides extensive details of its facilities, together with a variety of indexes.

The use of libraries and the internet should always be prior to the use of record offices and archives. You need to know what you are looking for in the latter before you use them, and you need to know whether you actually need to use them at all - has the information you need been published? Books and bibliographies should enable you to find out. Do not rush to the archives first; if you do, you risk subjecting unique documents to unnecessary wear and tear; you also risk wasting time finding information you could have found much more easily in books.

Record offices are usually - but not always - distinct from libraries, since the management of books requires quite different procedures to the management of archives: unique documents require much more care than books, and preservation rather than consultation is the main priority. There are a wide variety of record offices. Virtually all county authorities run a county record office, which houses the records of local government, and also acts as a place of deposit for parish records, local business and estate archives, school records, *etc.* The National Archives (formerly the Public Record Office) at Kew holds the archives of national government; it has, however, transferred census and probate records to the Family Records Centre, which it runs jointly with the Registrar General, and also holds indexes to the latter's civil registration records (see chapters 3, 7 & 8).

The web sites of many libraries and record offices are listed in the present author's *Family history on the web.* Addresses *etc.,* are updated every year in the annual *Family and local history handbook.* Library resources for family historians are listed on the *Familia* web site. *Archon* (on the National Archives website) is the authoritative web-based listing of record office sites. *A2A* provides on-line access to the archive catalogues of innumerable record offices, and should be checked by all genealogists. *Archives Hub* provides a similar index to the archival holdings of universities and colleges. The *National Register of Archives* (also on the National Archives site) holds some 43,000 unpublished lists of archival sources, which are indexed on its web site.

Many web-sites have been created by family history societies to provide information about their services and activities. Every family historian would be well-advised to join relevant societies. Well over 150 societies currently exist in England and Wales; most are members of the Federation of Family History Societies, and a full list appears on its web-site. The majority are concerned with research in particular places; there are also many one-name societies (which are mostly member societies of the Guild of One Name Studies - often referred to as the Goons), and a number with specialist interests such as the Quaker Family History Society and the Railway Ancestors Family History Society.

Virtually all societies publish a journal, which usually includes details of current events in the family history world, articles on their members' research, and details of members interests (which may also be published separately). These interest lists are particularly useful, as they can lead to invaluable exchanges of information with other researchers. Most societies have their own library, and many are engaged in the transcription and indexing of monumental inscriptions and other sources. Some have extensive publishing programmes (details are given by Hampson and Perkins). Regular meetings provide a means of meeting other researchers and learning about methods of research.

Web sites:

Gateways & Portals
- Genuki
  www.genuki.org.uk

- Cyndis List
  www.cyndislist.com

- Family History Online
  www.familyhistoryonline.net
  Databases of family history societies

Libraries
- Familia: the UK and Ireland's Guide to Genealogical Resources on the Web
  www.familia.org.uk

- OBI-OPACS in Britain and Ireland
  www.niss.ac.uk/lis/obi/obi.html
  Lists on-line library catalogues

Record Offices
- Archon
  www.archon.nationalarchives.gov.uk/
- Archives Hub
  www.archiveshub.ac.uk

- National Register of Archives
  www.nra.nationalarchives.gov.uk/

- A2A
  www.a2a.org.uk

- National Archives
  www.nationalarchives.gov.uk

Family History Societies
- Federation of Family History Societies
  www.ffhs.org.uk

- Family Search
  www.familysearch.org

Further Reading
Internet
- CHRISTIAN, PETER. *The Genealogists internet.* 2nd ed. Public Record Office, 2003
- RAYMOND, STUART A. *Family history on the web: an internet directory for England and Wales.* 3rd ed. F.F.H.S., 2004.
- HOWELLS, CYNDI. *Cyndi's list: a comprehensive list of 70,000 genealogy sites on the Internet.* 2nd ed. 2 vols. Baltimore: Genealogical Publishing Co., 2001. In late 2004, the website listed over 240,000 sites, and is expanding rapidly! New editions of the book are expected at regular intervals.

Books & Libraries

- RAYMOND, STUART A. *Using libraries: workshops for family historians.* F.F.H.S., 2001.

- RAYMOND, STUART A. *British genealogical library guides.* F.F.H.S., 1988- . (formerly *British genealogical bibliographies*). Includes many volumes listing resources for particular counties, as well as a number of national volumes.

- BROWN, LUCY M., & CHRISTIE, IAN R. *Bibliography of British history, 1789-1851.* Clarendon Press, 1977.

- HANHAM, H.J. *Bibliography of British history, 1851-1914.* Clarendon Press, 1976.

- PERKINS, JOHN P. *Current publications on microfiche for member societies.* 5th ed. F.F.H.S., 2002. Also available on CD.

- RAYMOND, STUART A. *British genealogy on microfiche.* F.F.H.S., 1999.

- RAYMOND, STUART A. *British family history on CD.* F.F.H.S., 2001.

- HAMPSON, ELIZABETH. *Current publications by member societies.* 10th ed. F.F.H.S., 1999.

- COLE, JEAN, & CHURCH, ROSEMARY. *In and around record repositories in Great Britain and Ireland.* 4th ed. A.B.M. Publishing, 1998. Detailed list of both record offices and libraries.

- BLATCHFORD, ROBERT, ed. *The family and local history handbook, incorporating the Genealogical services directory.* 8th ed. Robert Blatchford Publishing, 2004. New edition to be issued annually.

Chapter 2

Has it Been Done Before?

Has it been done before? Innumerable family histories and pedigrees have been compiled, and biographies are one of the most popular forms of light reading. Such works have an obvious importance for the family historian; if they are available, then you obviously need to know about them. Quite apart from their intrinsic interest for family members, it is likely that family histories in particular will include pedigrees and details of sources consulted. Biographies may also include a pedigree, and will almost certainly give details of close family. It is also worth finding out about works on other families who may have lived in the same areas as your ancestors; they may provide relevant information.

You may think it unlikely that there are any such works relating to your family. It is, however, always worth checking bibliographies and library catalogues for any that may have escaped your attention. The British Library holds an extensive collection of biographies and family histories; its catalogue is readily available on the internet, and printed catalogues of the British Museum (the British Library's predecessor) are available in most major reference libraries. The county volumes of Raymond's

British genealogical library guides provide extensive listings of family histories and pedigrees; biographies are listed at length in McColvin's bibliography and also in the *Bibliography of biography.* The many brief accounts of family history research printed in the journals of family history societies also ought to be checked; they are listed in the digest section of the Federation of Family History Societies journal, *Family history news & digest,* and in Raymond's county volumes.

Most entries in biographical dictionaries are likely to include details of parentage, spouse(s) and children. An extraordinarily wide range of such dictionaries is available; over 16,000 are listed by Slocum, and over 3,000,000 entries are indexed in the *Biography and genealogy master index.* The *Dictionary of national biography, Who's who,* and *Who was who* are the best known of such compilations, and are widely available in libraries, but there are also many others relating to specific groups of people. Some of those relating to particular occupations are discussed below (p. 104). Some relating to particular counties were published in the final years of the century, and are listed by Hanham.

Further Reading:
- RAYMOND, STUART A. *British genealogical library guides.* F.F.H.S., 1988- . See especially the county volumes, some of which are solely devoted to listings of family histories.

- McCOLVIN, L. R. *The librarian's subject guide to books. Vol.2. Biography, family history, genealogy, etc.* James Clarke & Co., 1960.
- *Bibliography of biography 1970-1984.* 40 fiche. British Library, 1985.
- SLOCUM, R. B. *Biographical dictionaries and related works: an international bibliography ...* 2nd ed. Gale Research, 1986.
- *Biography and genealogy master index: a consolidated index to more than 3,200,000 biographical sketches in over 350 current and retrospective biographical dictionaries.* 8 vols. Gale, 1980. Supplements 1981-5, 1986-9, and annually from 1990. Also available on CD.
- HANHAM, H. J. 'Neglected sources of biographical information: county biographical dictionaries, 1890-1937', *Bulletin of the Institute of Historical Research* **34**(89), 1961, 55-66.

Chapter 3

Civil Registration

The records of civil registration are the vital building blocks for anyone trying to construct a pedigree for their family in England & Wales since the beginning of the registration system in 1837. Different registration systems operated in Scotland, Ireland, the Isle of Man, and the Channel Islands; Wood provides a useful introduction to them. The information provided on birth, marriage and death certificates is likely to be the most useful official evidence that you will be able to find in drawing up your family tree. These certificates give the registration district, sub-district, year of registration, and the number of the entry in the register. They also give the information detailed below.

Birth Certificates
- 1. When and where born
- 2. Name if any
- 3. Sex
- 4. Name and surname of father
- 5. Name, surname and maiden surname of mother
- 6. Occupation of father
- 7. Signature, description, and residence of informant

- 8. When registered
- 9. Signature of registrar
- 10. Name entered after registration

The surname of the child was not given. It was assumed to be that of the father, unless the child was illegitimate. If that was the case, the mother could cause the name of the father to be inserted if she wished, up until 1875. Thereafter, the father had to appear personally at the registry office to certify his paternity. Otherwise, this space is left blank. If the father's name is entered, but the parents are not married, the child could take either of their surnames.

A time against the date of birth may indicate twins. Official records could be used to establish which twin was the eldest, and perhaps to settle questions of inheritance.

It is possible to obtain short birth certificates for administrative purposes. These are not of any use to the family historian, since they provide no indication of parentage.

Marriage Certificates
- Place of marriage
- When married
- Name and surname
- Age
- Condition (i.e. marital status)
- Rank or profession (if any)
- Residence at the time of marriage

- Father's name and surname
- Rank or profession of father
- Whether by banns, licence, or registrar's certificate (see chapter 4 for banns and licences)
- Signatures of parties, minister or registrar, and witnesses

Death Certificates
- 1. When and where died
- 2. Name and surname
- 3. Sex
- 4. Age (from June 1866)
- 5. Occupation
- 6. Cause of death
- 7. Signature, description and residence of informant
- 8. When registered
- 9. Signature of registrar

From 1874, the cause of death had to be certified by a doctor; hitherto, the cause given might be pure conjecture.

The authoritativeness of the information provided on certificates was dependent on the knowledge and reliability of informants. It was also dependent on the efficiency of the registrars and ministers who compiled the certificates. Much could go awry at this stage, as it could when the indexes to the civil registers were compiled. Detailed studies by Foster have demonstrated that both the original registers, and the indexes to them, are far from being free from error. Deliberate mis-information and copying errors are not uncommon, and will be discussed in more detail below. There is also the question of the extent to which under-registration occurred, especially in the early years of the system. That said, the records of civil registration do contain a vast amount of information useful to the genealogist. In order to obtain the relevant information, it is useful to know how the system worked, and continues to work.

Civil registration began on 1st July 1837. The county was divided into 619 districts (expanded to 623 in 1851), based on the recently formed poor law unions (see chapter 11). These districts were subsequently used for compiling the census (chapter 7). Full details of the areas covered by registration districts are given by Langston, and also on the 'Registration Districts' website. These districts were placed in the charge of a superintendant registrar, who had overall control of registrars in a number of sub-districts, and who initially frequently also served as clerk to the poor law guardians.

The registrars were required to compile registers of all births and deaths in their districts. Until 1874, the onus for registration of births and deaths was on the registrars, who were expected to travel around their sub-districts to record these events. Births had to be recorded within 42 days, deaths usually within five days. Informants were obliged to answer the registrar's questions, but not to actually report an event. Consequently, it has been estimated that, between 1837 and 1874, some 15 per cent of births went unregistered. From 1875, parents or the immediate family were required by law to report births and deaths. Quarterly returns had to be made of all births, marriages (see below), and deaths that had been registered in the quarter (these might include events which had occurred in an earlier quarter). These returns were copies of the original registers, rather than the originals themselves (the latter are still held in registry offices). The superintendent registrar had to certify registrars' returns as accurate before forwarding them to the registrar general.

Registrars were also empowered to conduct marriages and to maintain registers of marriages so conducted. However, most marriages continued to be religious ceremonies. Nonconformist and Roman Catholic chapels could be registered for marriages; however, until 1899, registrars had to be in attendance in order to register them. Most marriage registers were maintained by the Church of England; the Quakers and the Jews also kept them. They maintained duplicate registers, one for their own records, one for the district registry office when it was full. In a few instances, the original registers may still not be full, and hence still not in the registry office.

Church of England clergy, Jewish rabbis, and Quaker registering officers made their own quarterly returns of marriages to the Registrar General. These were made via superintendant registrars, but the latter did not have to certify their accuracy.

Superintendant registrars compiled their own indexes to birth and death registers, and also to the marriage registers compiled by registrars. Ecclesiastical registers, in general, were not indexed by them; the fact that they were usually kept by the church until they were full meant that they were not available for indexing - although there are exceptions to this rule. The district indexes may be more accurate than the General Register Office (G.R.O.) indexes, since they are based on the original registers, and there has been less chance for error to creep in. They are still held in district registry offices, where they may be consulted; if you know a particular event took place in a particular district, it may be better to check the local index first (unless it was a church marriage).

District registry offices should also hold 'marriage notice books'. These had the same purpose as banns, and originally were read three times at weekly meetings of boards of guardians; they were only used for registry office marriages, and enabled the proposed marriage to be challenged and forbidden if there was legal cause to do so.

Upon receipt of the quarterly returns from superintendent registrars, the G.R.O. compiled its own registers - which are consequently copies of copies, with all the potentialities for error that that implies. These registers were then indexed, and it is these indexes which most family historians must use in order to obtain birth, marriage and death certificates from the General Register Office.

There are three separate indexes: births, marriages and deaths. They were compiled quarterly, and against each person's name you will find the registration district, and the volume and page number of the entry in the registry. This information, together with the year and quarter of the volume consulted, is required in order to obtain a certificate. The original indexes are held by the Family Records Centre; and digital copies are available on two internet sites: 1837 Online (which charges a fee), and Free BMD (free but not yet complete). Microfiche and microfilm copies are also widely available in public libraries, Latter Day Saints Family History Centres, and some family history society libraries. The original volumes are heavy and awkward to handle; if this is likely to be a problem, then the internet or microfilm options may be preferable.

The indexes provide you with the basic information needed to apply for certificates. This includes the name of the person, the name of the registration district, and the volume and page number of the registered entry. You will also need the dates of the index. With this information, you can apply for a copy of the entry. The register itself cannot be consulted. Despite the fact that the original registers are in

London, the registers themselves are in Southport, and application must be made to:

> The General Register Office,
> Smedley Hydro,
> Trafalgar Road,
> Southport,
> PR8 2HH

Application forms are available at the Family Records Centre, and also online at the General Register Office site. It is possible to order certificates online, or by post. There is a fee for certificates.

A number of alternative courses of action may also be suggested. The General Register Office itself will search the indexes for you, or you can employ an agent to do so on your behalf. Reference has already been made to the indexes compiled by district registrars. If you know the district in which an event took place, then it is possible to obtain a certificate from the district registry office. As has already been suggested, their original registers, and their birth and death indexes, are likely to be superior in quality to those held by the General Register Office and Family Records Centre. However, bear in mind that the G.R.O. index references will not be of any use since they refer to a different register, even though it is derivative. Furthermore the superintendent registrar is likely to require more information to identify the original entry in the register than is the case with the G.R.O.; for example, it may be necessary to know the church at which a marriage took place.

Addresses for district registry offices are listed in Langston's *Handbook,* in the current edition of the *Family and local history handbook,* and on the *Registration Districts* website. This website also gives details of changes in boundaries to 1930.

Other civil registration information is also available on the internet. Projects are currently underway to create digitised indexes to the civil registers for a rapidly increasing number of counties and smaller areas; Cheshire led the way, but other entire counties are now being covered: Cambridgeshire, Derbyshire, Durham, Kent, Lancashire, Staffordshire, the West Midlands, and Yorkshire are all in progress, and more may have been added by the time you read this. These indexes are based on information provided by district registrars, and thus are likely to be more reliable than the G.R.O. indexes. They can be accessed via the FreeBMD site, which also acts as a gateway to other useful sites.

Many other sites are identified in the present author's *Births, Marriages and Deaths on the Web.* These may provide basic guidance, indexes, address lists, and / or information directly from registration certificates themselves. A number of family history societies and others maintain collections of certificates which members have acquired but do not need, and these are sometimes indexed; for an example, visit the U.K. BDM Exchange site.

Searching the civil registration indexes is not necessarily as straight-forward as might be expected. There are many reasons why an index entry may not be found. Deliberate mis-information by informants, errors in copying and indexing, and a range of other possibilities, all make the tasks of identifying certificates more complicated than might be expected.

The possibilities of errors in copying and indexing have been considered in great detail by Foster (although he has only researched the marriage index). It has to be remembered that the system was not designed with the demands of the genealogist in mind. The process of registration described above gave four chances for error to creep in: the initial registration, the copying of the entry by the district registrar, the copying of that copy for the main G.R.O. register, and the indexing of that register. Foster has shown how errors and omissions did creep in at all these stages, and that it is doubtful if the accuracy of the work was ever checked; he has concluded that there is a need 'for a complete overhaul' of the entire records. That is unlikely to happen, at least at government expense, although some indexes to district registrars registers are being revamped (see below). Genealogists need to be aware of the blemishes in the system.

A wide variety of other circumstances may also affect the location of an index entry, and the evidence provided by certificates. The requirements of the law, the literacy of informants, social customs, and unusual circumstances may all conspire to confuse the genealogist! It would be impossible to provide a comprehensive listing of the possibilities, but you may need to be aware of some of the following points:

- the date of registration is not the same as the date of the event, except in the case of marriage, which is normally registered immediately. Consequently, you may need to search the index for the quarter after a birth or death took place, or even later.
- the spelling of both surname and forename may not be what you expect. If you fail to find an entry, check as many variants of the spelling as you can think of, e.g. Smyth, Smythe, Smeath for Smith, Raymont, Raymond, Reyment for Raymond. Letters in names such as Whittington may be omitted, making Whitington or Witington; hand-writing might be mis-understood, so that capitals such as L, T, and S become confused. There are many possibilities. Fore-names may also be different; substituting Smith, Robert, for Smith, Bob, will place the index entry far away from where you expect to find it.
- a foundling child might have been given no surname at registration, and hence entered by forename only, after 'Z' in the births index.
- the place of birth given in a certificate is not necessarily the address of the mother, who may have gone home to her mother for the birth, or perhaps given birth in the workhouse or some other institution. In early certificates, only the parish may be given.

- children could be registered without a first name; even today that may be done. It may be that the child died at birth, or that it was to be adopted; it may be that the parents could not make up their minds!
- whether a child was named or not, it was possible to alter the name at baptism, provided the baptism took place within twelve months of registration. Such baptisms were not always reported to the registrar.
- a bride who was a widow was likely to use her married surname on her second marriage certificate. However, her status as a widow will also be noted, as will her father's surname.
- a still birth did not have to be registered until 1874. It is possible to find death certificates for babies who died without having their births registered.
- a bride who had changed her surname prior to marriage, e.g. to that of her step-father, should have used her current surname, and not her birth name, on her marriage certificate. Her father's surname will, however, also be given on the certificate.
- deaths did not necessarily take place at home. If people died whilst working or travelling away from home, their deaths may have been recorded in a totally unexpected registration district.
- the name of the deceased given on death certificates is the name by which they were known at the date of death, and not necessarily that used when their birth was registered. There are a multitude of

reasons why people might change their name, and such changes are not necessarily recorded officially.
- the event you are seeking may have taken place at sea or abroad.
- separate birth/baptism registers were maintained by the army.

Informants may have given incorrect or mis-leading information for a variety of reasons. Only a few can be suggested here:
- Births had to be registered within three weeks, later extended to six weeks. If parents were late registering, they might give a late date of birth to conceal their tardiness.
- Ages on marriage certificates may be false for a variety of reasons: a minor may have increased his age to conceal the need for parental consent; an old man may not have wanted his bride to know his true age.
- If both parties to a marriage lived in the same parish, it would have only been necessary to pay for banns to be read in one parish. Hence a false address may be given to avoid the necessity of paying for them to be read in two parishes
- Addresses on marriage certificates may have been temporary. The law required at least one partner in a marriage to be resident in a parish for four weeks before the marriage could take place in that parish's church. Hence one or both parties may have taken up temporary residence in order to

use a particular church, or perhaps given a false address.

- Occupations may be false or embellished to give a mis-leading impression of a person's status.
- Mothers of illegitimate children might conceal the fact of illegitimacy by registering the birth under the father's name, and claiming to be the father's wife.
- It was not unknown for grandmothers to register their daughter's illegitimate child as their own.
- The ages given on death certificates are open to much more suspicion than most other registration information. The dead person may not have known his own age, or he may have lied about it for much of his life. And he is not the person providing the information! If he did not know or lied, how likely is it that other informants (who may be quite unrelated, e.g. the master of a workhouse) would know?
- The cause of death given on death certificates might also be pure conjecture. Prior to 1874, the cause of death did not have to be certified by a doctor; informants might have only a vague idea, and consequently this entry is not to be trusted.

Finally, it should be noted that the whole system of civil registration is currently (late 2004) under review, and that a number of changes have been proposed which, if implemented, may require this chapter to be re-written for the next edition of this book. Full details of any changes will no doubt be given on the General Register Office website in due course.

Web Pages

- Civil Registration in England and Wales
  www.genuki.org.uk/big/eng/civreg/
  General advice

- Barbara's Registration Web Page: England and Wales Birth Marriage and Death Certificate Information
  home.clara.net/dixons/Certificates/indexbd.htm
  Detailed discussion of each entry on certificates

- England: Civil Registration
  www.genuki.org.uk/big/eng/CivilRegistration.html
  Links page

- The Family Records Centre
  www.familyrecords.gov.uk/frc/

- General Register Office
  www.gro.gov.uk

- FreeBMD
  www.freebmd.org.uk

- Registration Districts in England and Wales (1837-1930)
  www.fhsc.org.uk/genuki/REG/

- 1837 Online
  www.1837online.com/

- Ordering Birth Registration Certificates from England and Wales, using the Latter Day Saints Family History Centre's Resources
  www.oz.net/~markhow/ukbirths.htm

- UK BMD: Births, Marriages, Deaths and Censuses on the Internet
  www.ukbmd.org.uk/

- UK BDM Exchange
  www.ukbdm.co.uk

Further Reading
Basic Guides

- COLWELL, STELLA. *The Family Records Centre: a users guide.* 2nd ed. P.R.O. Users Guide **17.** Public Record Office, 2002.
- McLAUGHLIN, EVE. *Civil registration of births marriages and deaths.* Rev. ed. Haddenham: Varneys Press, 2001.
- RAYMOND, STUART A. *Births, Marriages and Deaths on the Web.* 2 vols. Bury: F.F.H.S., 2002.
- WOOD, TOM. *British civil registration.* 2nd ed. An introduction to ... series. Bury: F.F.H.S., 2000.
- *Using birth, marriage, and death records.* Pocket guide to family history. Public Record Office, 2000.

More Specialist Works

- NISSEL, MURIEL. *People count: a history of the General Register Office.* H.M.S.O., 1987.

- FOSTER, MICHAEL WHITFIELD. *"A comedy of errors",
  or, the marriage records of England and Wales,
  1837-1899.* Wellington, New Zealand: Michael W.
  Foster, 1998.
- FOSTER, MICHAEL WHITFIELD. *"A comedy of errors",
  act 2.* Wellington, New Zealand: Michael Whitfield
  Foster, 1999.

Registration Districts

- LANGSTON, BRETT. *A handbook to the civil
  registration districts of England and Wales.*
  Northwich: B. Langston, 2001.
- WIGGINS, RAY. *Registration districts: an alphabetical
  list of over 650 districts, with details of counties,
  sub-districts, and adjacent districts.* Society of
  Genealogists Enterprises, 2001.

Chapter 4

Parish Registers and other Records Of Births Marriages And Deaths

One of the effects of the introduction of civil registration was to reduce the importance of ecclesiastical registers for genealogists. Opposition to the introduction of civil registration had been based on the opinion that it would reduce the numbers marrying in church, that there would be no need to register baptisms, and that it would lead to a decline in religious observance. These views were prophetic of what was to come; however, registration was not the cause. Religious observance continued much as before for most of the century, and hence ecclesiastical registers continued to record as many events as before 1837. It was only in the twentieth century, with the increasing secularization of society, that the proportion of weddings celebrated in church, and the number of children baptised, fell dramatically.

Consequently, ecclesiastical registers for the nineteenth century contain as much information of use to the family historian as those for earlier centuries; indeed, more. Rose's Act of 1812 (see below), and the implementation of civil registration itself, actually rendered parish registers more useful than they had been before.

The major advantages of civil registration over ecclesiastical registers is the nation-wide coverage of a (suspect) national index, and the comprehensive coverage of civil registers at both district and national levels. These two advantages reduce the need to search innumerable ecclesiastical registers for similar information. However, if the civil indexes fail to yield the desired information, or if the church in which a particular event took place is known, or can be reasonably guessed at, then the ecclesiastical registers should be consulted. They may also be consulted if information from civil registration is questionable.

The term 'ecclesiastical registers' encompasses both Church of England parish registers, and nonconformist registers. The keeping of the former is governed by acts of Parliament. The two acts of most significance prior to 1837 were Lord Hardwicke's Marriage Act, 1754, and Rose's Act, 1812, which governed the keeping of baptism and burial registers.

Church of England Marriage Registers
Hardwicke's Act required all marriages to take place in the parish church of one of the parties (although it only required three weeks residence for a party to be legally considered 'of this parish'). Jews and Quakers were exempted from this requirement, since they already kept adequate registers. The act also required banns to be called on three successive Sundays in the

parish church(es) of both parties, in order to give an adequate opportunity for objections to be made to the marriage. Alternatively, a marriage licence could be obtained from the ecclesiastical authorities. Detailed regulations were laid down for the keeping of both marriage and banns registers. Entries for marriages were supposed to include the date of marriage, the names of the spouses, their parish(es) of residence, their marital status, whether the marriage was by banns or licence, and the groom's occupation. The Register had to be signed by both spouses, by two witnesses, and by the officiating clergyman. In some churches, it was the custom for churchwardens or the parish clerk to act as witnesses; however, frequently the witnesses were relatives of the spouses, and this information may consequently prove useful to the genealogist. Usually, the register was kept in a book specially printed with forms for the purpose.

Banns

Banns registers were often kept in the same book as the marriage registers; the form for entering marriages might also include space for details of banns, or there might be a separate section for banns at the back of the book. Alternatively, some parishes kept a separate banns register. After the introduction of civil registration, a separate banns register was required. It is always worth checking the banns register; it may well reveal additional information. Banns were called in the parishes of both spouses, and may therefore be used to locate the place of marriage if it took place elsewhere. If an objection to the marriage was made, it may be recorded. Banns registers record intended marriages; there is no guarantee that the marriage actually took place.

Hardwicke's Act required parties to give the parish a written notice to publish banns. This requirement was often waived due to illiteracy, but occasionally such notices survive amongst parish records, and may provide additional information.

Church of England Marriage Registers & Civil Registration

The introduction of civil registration increased the amount of information found in parish registers. Henceforth, the Registrar General supplied each parish with two books of printed forms, each of which had to be completed for each marriage. One was kept by the parish, the other was to be returned to the district registrar when it had been filled up. The information provided in these books is discussed in chapter 3; here it is worth noting that this system means that you are able to consult the original registers for all church marriages, whereas you cannot directly consult the registers held by the Registrar General. The registers retained by the church are, in any case, likely to be much more reliable; there has been much less possibility of error creeping in during copying processes.

Church of England Baptism and Burial Registers

Until 1812, there was no regulation of the form of entries for baptism and burial entries in parish registers. Often the barest information was given: dates and names only. The dates of baptisms were given, rather than dates of birth. Baptism entries usually recorded the name of the father, and sometimes the mother; burial entries simply the name of the deceased.

Rose's Act, 1812, required the use of separate registers for baptisms and burials; they were to be kept in specially printed books, in the same way as marriage registers had been kept for half a century. The forms used for baptismal entries gave space to enter the date, christian name(s), the names of both parents, the place of abode (usually more than just the name of the parish), the 'quality, trade, or profession' of the father, and the name of the clergyman who conducted the ceremony. For burials, the name, abode, place of burial, age, and the name of the clergyman involved were required. These were minimal requirements; more information may be found.

Civil registration had no impact on the keeping of parish registers of baptisms and burials, although a few clergymen may have discouraged parents from reporting births to the registrar in the early years of the system.

Bishop's Transcripts
In 1800, copies of parish registers were still being returned annually to the bishop of each diocese, as they had been for the previous two centuries. After the passing of Rose's Act 1812 they were written on printed sheets in the same format as was now being used for the original registers; they were supposed to be precise copies. The advent of civil registration in 1837 meant that transcripts of marriage registers had to be sent to the registrar; consequently they ceased to be sent to the bishop. However, transcripts of the baptism and burial registers continued to be made for bishops. This practice began to die out in mid-century; however, bishops transcripts as late as 1907 are known.

Other Copies
The transcription and indexing of parish registers by family historians is proceeding apace. Many editions have been published by record societies and parish register societies, although unfortunately these mostly end in 1812 or 1837. Some of these are now available on CD. Family history societies have published many transcripts on microfiche, including some that reach into the late nineteenth century. Comprehensive listings of published parish registers are provided in the county volumes of Raymond's *British genealogical library guides*. The guides by Perkins and Hampson (see p. 19) should also be checked. Many web pages are devoted to transcripts and indexes of parish registers;

these are listed in Raymond's *Births, marriages and deaths on the web.* Numerous unpublished transcripts are held in local history libraries and record offices, by family history societies, and especially by the Society of Genealogists (see its catalogue below). Transcribers will often make three copies, one for each of these organisations. The majority of these transcripts pre-date the nineteenth-century, but it is worth checking to see whether relevant transcripts are available. Comprehensive listings are given in the county volumes of the *National index of parish registers.*

It should be added that an increasing number of record offices are now making their parish registers available on microfilm/fiche, and sometimes offering copies for sale. It would be extremely useful if they could be persuaded to use CD's for this purpose; only a handful of facsimiles of original registers are currently available in this way, although CD's are being used increasingly to re-print transcripts published in the late nineteenth and early twentieth centuries.

The existence of a transcript does not make it unnecessary to check the original, but may make it easier to locate the entries sought. Researchers should be aware that, whilst many transcripts are excellent, others are woefully inaccurate.

Parish Register Indexes

There have been a variety of attempts to index parish registers. There is not, however, a totally comprehensive index, and most end in 1812 or 1837. A large proportion of registers remain unindexed. It is important to be aware that indexes are just that: indexes. They are not the original source, neither are they transcripts of it, and they may not include all the information found in the original source. Their value is entirely dependent on the quality of the document being indexed; the latter may be a very poor transcript. It is also dependent on the accuracy of the indexer, which also cannot be guaranteed. No index can be 100% accurate. It is therefore necessary for the researcher to check index entries which seem to be relevant against the original registers (which have not necessarily been seen by the indexer, who may have used a transcript). The original source may reveal additional information, and will certainly reveal any indexing and transcribing errors. A healthy degree of scepticism is a useful attribute for researchers.

The most important index is undoubtedly the English portion of the *International Genealogical Index*. This is widely available in public libraries, record offices, and family history societies, on both microfilm and CD's; the CD version is known as the *British Isles vital records index*. The index can also be searched on the internet at the Family Search website.

The I.G.I., as it is known, is not simply an index to parish registers. It also indexes 'family record sheets' which have been submitted by patrons, and which provide pedigree information. The accuracy of the latter is entirely dependent on the contributor. Each entry in the index gives a name, the type, date, and place of the event, and the batch number of the source, together with 'Temple ordinances' information only of relevance to the Latter Day Saints, who are responsible for the index. The batch numbers are important, as they enable a copy of the source indexed to be obtained through any of the Latter Day Saints Family History Centres. You should always check this; it may be a microfilm of the original register, in which case you may have found the information you need. If, on the other hand, it is simply a transcript, in an ideal world you should check the original register.

The I.G.I., unlike some other indexes, does include information for the whole of the nineteenth century. However, it only indexes baptisms and marriages; burials are excluded. They are now being covered by the *National burial index for England and Wales*. This is a co-operative venture by member societies of the Federation of Family History Societies; the second edition, on four CD's, includes 14,000,000+ records, many relating to the nineteenth century, and a new edition is planned every three years. Parts of the index for particular counties are available on the internet at the Family History Online website, on a pay per view basis.

Another useful aid is provided by Boyd's marriage index. This was originally compiled directly from original parish registers, bishops' transcripts, and marriage licences (see below), and has entries for most counties, with almost complete coverage for East Anglia. However, there are no entries post-1840. The original typescript index is held by the Society of Genealogists, and copies are available in a handful of other institutions. However, the index has been digitised and is available on a pay per view basis at the British Origins website.

Pallot's marriage index is a similar private index. The majority of entries relate to the London and Middlesex areas; however, there are some entries from most counties, including Wales. Its coverage only extends from 1780 to 1837. It was begun in the early nineteenth century and includes information from a handful of registers which have since been destroyed. The original index is held by the Institute of Heraldic & Genealogical Studies in Canterbury; it has, however, been digitised, and can be searched via the internet on a pay per view basis.

A wide range of other indexes to parish registers are available. A number created by (mainly) family history societies are available on the *Family History Online* web site. Others have been published by family history societies and commercial organisations such as Original Indexes (for Northumberland and Durham). Professional genealogists, family history societies, and other organisations hold many unpublished indexes; these can be tracked down by consulting the two Gibson guides listed below, or by contacting local family history societies for information. Most indexes are listed in *Phillimore's atlas and index of parish registers,* and in the county volumes of the *National index of parish registers.*

Locating Parish Registers and Transcripts

Most original parish registers are now deposited in the relevant county record offices, although they may still be with the incumbent if they are still in use. Record offices frequently publish lists of the registers they hold, and their web-sites may contain information about such publications - or, in some cases, the lists themselves. At the national level, the *Phillimore atlas and index of parish registers* provide a summary list of the availability and location of all parish registers, together with very useful maps of the boundaries of ancient parishes, juxtaposed with county maps originally published in the nineteenth century. Much more detailed information on original registers, bishops transcripts, and modern transcripts is available in the county volumes of the *National index of parish registers,* which also covers non-conformist registers. Detailed lists of published parish registers are provided in the county volumes of Raymond's *British genealogical library guides* - although, as already noted, these often only run to 1812 or 1837. Many are also listed in the Society of Genealogists published catalogue.

Marriage Licences

If a couple wished to marry without waiting for the calling of the banns, or preferred to avoid the publicity that banns would cause, they could obtain a marriage licence from bishops, archbishops, or those responsible in peculiar jurisdictions. Licences do not usually survive; however, the 'allegations' which had to be submitted when applying for a licence may usually be found in diocesan record offices, as may the bonds - sworn statements - that had to be made by friends or relatives until 1823, confirming that they knew of no impediment to the marriage, that it would take place in a specified church, and that those who swore to the bond would forfeit a specified sum if the licence were misused. There may also be licence registers. If a marriage that is known to have taken place cannot be traced in civil or parish registers, it may be that these records could help. Conversely, however, the fact that a licence was issued does not necessarily prove that it was used.

Some marriage licence records have been published; a full listing of published and unpublished records is provided by Gibson. Published abstracts and indexes are also listed in Raymond's county bibliographies.

Other Church of England Records

Parish registers are not the only Church of England records likely to be of interest to genealogists. Many other parish, archdeaconry, and diocesan records may also provide useful information. At parish level, civil and ecclesiastical government were closely intertwined, and at archdeaconry and diocesan level the church continued to exercise probate jurisdiction until 1858. Records relating to the relief of the poor are discussed in chapter 11; wills in chapter 8; rates in chapter 14.

Vestry minutes survive for many parishes in the nineteenth century, and cover a wide variety of topics. From 1818 they were legally required to be kept. Matters such as the appointment of parish officers, the allocation of pews, poor law issues, *etc.,* were dealt with, and many names were recorded. Churchwardens accounts record expenditure for a wide range of purposes: payments to the sexton, the parish clerk, the bell-ringers; the relief of the poor; the maintainance of the church, the eradication of vermin, *etc.* A wide variety of other records may also be available from the parish chest: deeds and rentals relating to church property, lists of contributors to various funds, charity records, tithe and enclosure records (see chapter 16), *etc.*

A wide range of records are also available in the diocesan archives. Nineteenth century clergy can usually be traced through printed sources; they can also be traced through diocesan records of institutions and ordinations, and through licences for curates *etc.* Ecclesiastical licences for teachers continued to be issued until the 1850's. The bishops continued to hold visitations, generating presentments by the churchwardens, replies to bishops queries (some of which have been published) and visitation returns, all of which may identify clergymen, churchwardens and others. Terriers listing church property continued to be drawn up, sometimes mentioning many names. Faculties were issued for matters to do with church fabric. Meeting House licences continued to be issued until mid-century, authorising the use of nonconformist buildings for worship. Church courts continued to sit at both archidiaconal and diocesan levels; their remit was not as wide as it had been in previous centuries, but their records may still be worth examining.

Web Sites
- Boyd's Marriage Index, 1538-1840
  www.britishorigins.com/help/
  popup-aboutbo-bmi2.htm

- Pallot's Marriage Index, 1780-1837
  www.ancestry.com/search/rectype/vital/
  pallot/mainmarriage.htm

- Family Search
  www.familysearch.org

- What is the I.G.I.?
  www.livgenmi.com/fhcigi.htm

Further Reading
General
- COX, J. CHARLES. *The parish registers of England.* Methuen & Co., 1910.
- GIBBENS, LILIAN. *Church registers.* An introduction to ... series. F.F.H.S., 1994.
- *Using birth, marriage and death records.* Pocket guides to family history. Public Record Office, 2000.

Lists & Indexes

- *National index of parish registers.* Society of Genealogists, 1973-. Many general and county volumes. Comprehensive guide.
- HUMPHERY-SMITH, CECIL R. *Phillimore atlas and index of parish registers.* 3rd ed. Phillimore, 2003.
- GIBSON, JEREMY, & HAMPSON, ELIZABETH. *Marriage and census indexes for family historians.* 7th ed. F.F.H.S., 1998.
- GIBSON, JEREMY. *Bishops transcripts and marriage licences, bonds and allegations: a guide to their location and indexes.* 5th ed. F.F.H.S., 2001.
- GIBSON, JEREMY, & HAMPSON, ELIZABETH. *Specialist indexes for family historians.* 2nd ed. F.F.H.S., 2000.
- *Parish register copies in the library of the Society of Genealogists.* 11th ed. Society of Genealogists, 1995.
- RAYMOND, STUART. *Births, marriages and deaths on the web.* 2 vols. F.F.H.S., 2002. New edition in preparation.
- *British Isles vital records index.* 16 C.D.'s. 2002.
- *National Burial Index for England and Wales.* 4 CDs. 2nd ed. F.F.H.S., 2004.

Other Records

- TATE, W.E. *The parish chest: a study of the records of parochial administration in England.* 3rd ed. Phillimore, 1983. Reprint of 1969 edition.
- BOURNE, SUSAN, & CHICKEN, ANDREW H. *Records of the Church of England: a practical guide for the family historian.* The authors, 1991.

Chapter 5

Nonconformist and Roman Catholic Registers and Records

The religious census of 1851 revealed that the numbers attending Church of England services were fewer than those who attended other churches. This fact is reflected to a certain extent in the records of other denominations, although for various reasons some of their members may be recorded in Church of England registers. For example, only Quakers and Jews could legally be married by their own ceremonies prior to 1837; otherwise, marriages conducted outside of the Church of England were legally invalid. Indeed, nonconformist registers generally were often not accepted by the courts, government departments, and the armed forces, despite an act of 1785 which established their validity. Burial could be problematic for nonconformists, who frequently did not have their own burial grounds; it was not until 1880 that nonconformist burial services were permitted in parish churchyards. Some nonconformists - especially the Methodists - actually preferred to use Church of England ceremonies for baptism and marriage. After the introduction of civil registration in 1837, which was seen as a great victory by the nonconformists, most of their churches did not bother to keep marriage registers. Their churches could be registered for marriages, but until 1898 each marriage had to be attended by a registrar, who entered it in the civil registers.

Despite these caveats, many nonconformist and Roman Catholic registers do exist, although they are far fewer in number than Church of England registers. Control over their format and content was minimal, apart from that which was exercised by some of the denominations themselves. There was no equivalent to the detailed regulations laid down for Church of England registers by Hardwicke's Act and Rose's Act, as described in chapter 4. Nevertheless, there was government concern for the authenticity and safe-keeping of the registers. At the same time as civil registration was established, a Registration Commission was set up to inquire into their 'state, custody and authenticity'. Churches were invited to surrender their registers to the commission, who would authenticate them and deposit them with the General Register Office, where they would be available for inspection. Over 6,000 registers were deposited; c.300 more came in when a second request was issued in 1857, and another 150 were received during the rest of the century. These registers are now in the National Archives, class RG4 and may be consulted on microfilm; the List and Index Society has published a full listing. The Quaker registers are in RG 8.

Many churches were reluctant to hand their registers over to the Commission; the Roman Catholics in particular generally refused to do so. Most of the registers which were retained by churches have, however, now been deposited in county record offices, as have those which were compiled after 1837. The *National index of parish registers* provides full details of the availability and location of these registers. However, its listing of the registers of burial grounds, which were required by law from 1864, is not as comprehensive; some of these have been deposited in record offices; other are still with burial ground custodians.

There were considerable variations in record keeping between the various denominations; both the structure of particular denominations, and their theology, affected the records that were kept. Baptism, for example, is not practised by Quakers; Baptists, however, baptise adults, and not infants. Quaker meetings maintain close ties with each other, and their records are much more centralised than those of the Congregationalists, whose churches were independent of any central control. These variations need to be kept in mind when searching denominational records, and a brief outline of the record-keeping practices of the major denominations may prove useful.

Quakers

Quakers originated in the religious upheavals of the mid-seventeenth century, and have maintained detailed records of their members ever since. Their 'meetings' comprised the local 'preparative' meeting relating to a single congregation, the 'monthly meeting', which had responsibility for the membership and property of several preparative meetings, the 'quarterly meeting', covering roughly a single county, and the 'yearly meeting' for the whole of England.

Until 1837, the monthly meetings used printed books to record births (not baptisms), marriages, and burials. That ceased on 30th June 1837, and most of these registers were surrendered to the Registrar General as already mentioned. However, before they were surrendered, digests were made from the registers in duplicate; one was retained by the Quarterly Meeting, the other was sent to the yearly meeting, and are now in Friends House Library, Euston Road, London NW1 2BJ. The former may have been deposited in county record offices; the latter has been microfilmed and may be consulted in major reference libraries.

From 1st July 1837, monthly meetings were required to appoint their own registering officers for marriages; they were responsible for keeping duplicate marriage registers on forms supplied by the Registrar General, just as Church of England clergymen did. In addition, a new form of birth note and burial note was adopted. In 1860, digests were again prepared from these notes and from the marriage register, and continued throughout the nineteenth century; these digests are at Friends House Library. The original notes may have been deposited in county record offices.

In addition to the registers, Quakers also kept a variety of other records which might provide useful information. Official lists of members were maintained. Minutes of meetings contain many names; those of Monthly meetings record Friends who were moving to another Meeting, who were 'acknowledged' as 'ministers', who were disowned (and perhaps re-instated) for offences such as drunkenness, being absent, and paying tithes. Quakers were not supposed to pay tithes, and were liable to suffer in consequence; their sufferings were recorded in 'books of sufferings'. Many records have been deposited in county record offices.

Congregationalists, Presbyterians (and Unitarians) and Baptists

These denominations can be considered together, since their record-keeping practices were quite similar. The government of all their churches was based in practice upon the church meeting, and the central structures had little or no control over individual congregations, or over their record keeping. Until 1837, they generally maintained registers of baptisms (or births for the Baptists); after that date, they usually ceased to maintain marriage registers, at least until 1898. As already noted, however, they were required to maintain registers for their own burial grounds from 1864. Nonconformist births/baptisms were also recorded in a national register established by the Protestant Dissenting Deputies in 1742. This was wound up in 1837, and is now held by the National Archives (RG5). There is an index in RG 4/4652-76. Over 50,000 births were recorded. Most pre-1837 registers were surrendered to the Registration Commission; they are recorded in the List & Index Society volume mentioned above. Various lists of these surrendered registers, of post-1837 registers, and of surviving registers which were not surrendered, are given in the works by Breed, Clifford and Ruston. Many have now been deposited in county record offices; however, some are still with church officers, or have been deposited with denominational organizations such as the Strict Baptist Historical Society (see Breed for details). Full listings of their surviving registers are also given in the county volumes of the *National index of parish registers.*

Other records of these churches may also be available. Minute books record the affairs of particular congregations, and sometimes note that requests for baptisms or marriages were granted. Most congregations maintained a membership register, which, if it can be found, may provide useful information such as both maiden and married surnames of ladies, or addresses.

A small collection of archives from these churches is held by Dr. Williams' Library, 14, Gordon Square,

London W.C.1., which also holds a substantial collection of nonconformist literature, including many histories of individual churches, and a variety of journals, both historical and contemporary. The latter often include notices of births, marriages and deaths, and of ministerial movements, as well as obituaries.

Methodists

Methodism was a product of the eighteenth century, inspired by the teachings of the Wesley brothers and others. In the nineteenth century, the movement was split between a number of separate denominations: The Methodist New Connexions split from the parent body in 1797, the Primitive Methodists in 1807, the Bible Christians in 1815, the Protestant Methodists in 1827 and the Wesleyan Methodists in 1836. The two latter groups merged to form the United Methodist Free Church in 1857, but it was not until the twentieth century that all these groups re-united.

All of these denominations had the same basic administrative structure. At the bottom were the individual chapels, which ran their own affairs, but shared their ministers with the other chapels in the circuit. There might be fifteen or twenty chapels in a circuit, served by two or three full-time ministers and a number of lay preachers. Circuits came together into districts, and at the top of the heirarchy was the Conference. Family historians are primarily interested in the records created by chapel and circuit, which have normally been deposited in county record offices.

In the nineteenth century, Methodists kept registers of births or baptisms, and sometimes deaths or burials. However, Methodist baptisms often took place in the parish church, and are recorded in parish registers. Prior to 1837, marriages could only legally be conducted by Church of England clergymen; thereafter they were registered by the local registrar. Consequently, Methodist marriage registers were not kept until 1898. Baptismal registers were sometimes kept at chapel level, sometimes at circuit level. Most of those pre-dating 1837 were deposited with the Registration Commission; after that date registers are most likely to be in county record offices, although some may remain with ministers. They are listed in the county volume of the *National index of parish registers;* Leary lists those in the National Archives, and also copies held by the Society of Genealogists. Burial and death registers are similarly located and listed; however, not many are available, especially from before 1864, when legislation was enacted requiring the maintainance of registers for burial grounds.

Some births and baptisms were also recorded at national level. The Methodist General Registry (also known as the Metropolitan Wesleyan Registry) was established by the Wesleyans in 1818, and recorded c.10,000 entries (some dating back to 1773) before it was wound up in 1834. This record is now held in the National Archives (RG 5), with an index in RG 4/4677-80.

A wide variety of other Methodist records can be found. At local level, minutes of circuits, chapels, and local preachers meetings all contain many names. Class books list members, circuit plans name those who preached. A variety of other documents may have been deposited in county record offices.

The records of the Methodist Conference have been deposited in the Methodist Archives and Research Centre, which also holds numerous collections of related archives and papers, including the personal papers of c.4,000 ministers (although not circuit and chapel records). It also holds an extensive collection of chapel histories, and runs of many Methodist journals and newspapers. The latter often contain obituaries, notes on movements of clergy, personal announcements, *etc.* The Centre's website includes an index of ministers and a biographical index.

At the very end of the nineteenth century, the Wesleyan Methodist Conference launched their 20th Century Fund, in order to build Westminster Central Hall. Between 1898 and 1904 this fund attracted subscriptions from over 1,000,000 subscribers. Their names were inscribed on a 'historic roll', which is virtually a census of the denomination's membership, plus many others. The roll is on display at Westminster Central Hall.

Roman Catholics

By 1800, the legal disabilities under which Roman Catholics had suffered since the Reformation had largely disappeared. Their numbers began to swell in the 1840's, with the conversion of upper class Anglicans, the influx of Irish refugees, especially during the famine years, and the activities of Italian missionaries amongst the working classes in the Midlands and South. Dioceses were established in 1850, but parishes were not created until the twentieth century. Priests created their own 'missions', many of which became permanent in the nineteenth century. They maintained their own registers of baptisms, marriages and burials. Legally, before 1837 they had to marry in an Anglican church, but sometimes a Roman Catholic ceremony was also conducted, and might be recorded in their registers. After 1837, they often continued to maintain their own marriage registers, although the civil registrars also recorded them in the same way as they recorded nonconformist marriages. Gandy has listed all missions prior to 1880, with their surviving registers. Lists of registers may also be found in the county volumes of the *National index of parish registers.* Many transcripts have been deposited in the Catholic Central Library.

Anstruther has indexed Catholic marriages c.1750-1880 and baptisms 1795-1888, mainly from London and Essex. A number of Catholic registers have been published by the Catholic Record Society, who have also edited a variety of other records which may be of use. Gandy's various bibliographies list these and many other publications.

Web Pages
Baptists
- Baptist Historical Society
  www.baptisthistory.org.uk

- Strict Baptist Historical Society
  www.strictbaptisthistory.org.uk

Methodists
- Methodist Archives and Research Centre
  rylibweb.man.ac.uk/data1/dg/text/method.html

Quakers
- Friends House Library
  www.quaker.org.uk/library/

- Quaker Family History Society
  www.rootsweb.com/"engqfhs/

Roman Catholics
- Catholic Family History Society
  www.catholic-history.org.uk/cfhs/

- Catholic Record Society
  www.catholic-history.org.uk/crs/

- Catholic Central Library
  www.catholic-library.org.uk

Further Reading
- STEEL, D.J. *Sources for nonconformist genealogy and family history.* National index of parish registers **2**. Society of Genealogists, 1973.

- STEEL, D.J., & SAMUEL, EDGAR. *Sources for Roman Catholic and Jewish genealogy and family history.* National index of parish registers **3.** Phillimore, for the Society of Genealogists, 1974.
- SHORNEY, DAVID. *Protestant nonconformity and Roman Catholicism: a guide to sources in the Public Record Office.* P.R.O. Readers guide **13.** P.R.O. Publications, 1996.
- MULLETT, M. *Sources for the history of English nonconformity, 1660-1830.* Archives & the user **8.** British Records Association, 1991.
- *General Register Office: registers of births, marriages and deaths, surrendered to the non-parochial registers commissions RG 4 and RG 8.* 2 vols. List and Index Society **265-6.** 1996. Supersedes the Society's vol. **42.**

Baptists
- BREED, GEOFFREY R. *My ancestors were Baptists: how can I find out more about them?* 4th ed. Society of Genealogists, 2002.

Congregationalists
- CLIFFORD, DAVID J.H. *My ancestors were Congregationalists in England and Wales. How can I find out more about them?* Society of Genealogists, 1997.

Methodists
- LEARY, WILLIAM. *My ancestors were Methodists. How can I find out more about them?* 2nd ed. Society of Genealogists, 1990.

Presbyterians/Unitarians

- RUSTON, A. *My ancestors were Presbyterians / Unitarians. How can I find out more about them?* 2nd ed. Society of Genealogists, 2001.

Quakers

- MILLIGAN, EDWARD H. *My ancestors were Quakers: how can I find out more about them?* [New ed.] Society of Genealogists, 1999.
- *General Register Office. Society of Friends registers, notes and certificates of births, marriages and deaths (RG 6).* List & Index Society **267**. 1996.
- *Friends House Library digest registers of births, marriages and burials for England and Wales, 17th c. - 1837.* 32 microfilm reels. World Microfilm Publications, 1989.

Roman Catholics

- GANDY, M. *Tracing your Catholic ancestors in England.* Basic facts about ... series. F.F.H.S., 1998.
- GANDY, M. *Catholic missions and registers.* 6 vols. + atlas vol. Michael Gandy, 1993.
- GANDY, MICHAEL. *Catholic family history: a bibliography of general sources.* The author, 1996.
- GANDY, MICHAEL. *Catholic family history: a bibliography of local sources.* Michael Gandy, 1996.
- ANSTRUTHER, GODFREY. *Catholic baptism index.* Fiche. Miscellaneous series **7**. Parish Register Transcription Society, 2003.

- ANSTRUTHER, GODFREY. *Catholic marriage index.* Fiche. Miscellaneous series **6.** Parish Register Transcription Society, 2003.

Chapter 6

Monumental Inscriptions

Churches, churchyards and cemeteries are full of monuments with inscriptions memorializing the dead. The custom of erecting tombstones and other memorials has been practised for centuries. In the nineteenth century, however, the cost of such memorials was reduced by more efficient transport - canals and railways - and came within reach of the mass market. Consequently, the number of memorials increased dramatically over previous centuries, as the lower classes copied their betters.

The progress of urbanisation also had an impact on burial practices. Many urban churchyards, especially in London, were full to overflowing, by the end of the eighteenth century, and many had to be closed to new burials. The inability of the church to provide sufficient space for new burials resulted in the opening up of many private cemeteries; e.g. Brookwood Cemetery, near Woking, which had its own private railway and covered no less than 2000 acres. Some of the smaller private cemeteries attracted much criticism, and many local councils took matters into their own hands and established municipal cemeteries. This activity was greatly encouraged by a series of burial acts in the 1850's.

A high proportion of nineteenth-century Britons were, therefore, buried in municipal and private cemeteries, rather than in churchyards, and that is often where their memorials may be found, although country churchyards continued - and continue - to be used. Genealogists need to be aware that the study of these memorials is a sub-discipline of the history of sculpture, and that there are many studies of memorial stones as works of art; Kemp is a recent example. The design of memorial stones was often influenced by the Greek revival in the early nineteenth century; this was followed by the Gothic revival later in the century. Memorials were not only in stone; there was also a revival of memorial brasses placed in churches, and, to a lesser extent, of stained glass windows.

The genealogist is primarily concerned with the information to be found in inscriptions. The sculpture itself, however, should not be neglected; its quality and elaborateness may indicate the social status of the deceased, and the tools of his trade or profession may be sculpted even if his occupation is not given in the inscription. The information given in inscriptions varies greatly; name and date of death or burial are the bare minimum, but much more may be added - residence, (including previous residences), place of death, occupation, name of the spouse, parentage, *etc., etc.* There may be an extensive epitaph which may or may not be informative; if several members of the same family are buried in the same plot it may be possible to construct a more or less extensive pedigree from one tombstone. If a tombstone is found, a check should aways be made to see whether there are any others for the same family in the immediate vicinity; there often are. It should be noted that not all inscriptions necessarily relate to burials in the same place.

Memorial inscriptions often provide more information than the entries in civil and parish registers, although this tended to decrease as the century progressed. They should be copied in full by the researcher, together with details of any interesting engravings such as the tools of the deceased's trade, or coats of arms. It must, however, be borne in mind that inscriptions are as liable to error as any other source, especially in view of the fact that they may not have been erected for a year or two after the deceased's death. The information they give should always be carefully compared with the information in the burial register, and in the other sources discussed in this book.

Locating the grave is not always easy. It may not be too much of a problem in a small churchyard, but may be more difficult in larger cemeteries. However, plans of cemeteries are often to be found in local record offices, or in the cemetery's own office. This, perhaps in conjunction with the burial register, should enable one to locate the grave more easily.

Graves do not necessarily have tombstones, and almost certainly will not if the deceased was a pauper. That said, many, perhaps most, do, and it is probable that at least some of your nineteenth-century forebears were commemorated in this way. However, the condition of tombstones varies greatly, and the inscriptions on them are not always easy to read. Some churchyards and cemeteries have been well looked after. Others are badly neglected, with tombstones covered in lichen and surrounded by long grass. Wind, rain, and pollution can do a great deal of damage to inscriptions, as can vandalism. Some stones have been moved to make way for re-development, or to enable the grass to be mowed more easily. Some have been lost altogether. Fortunately many copies of inscriptions have been made. Inscriptions from burial grounds which have been re-developed are likely to have been recorded; the names on tombstones, and often the entire inscriptions, may be recorded in files held by the National Archives, class RG37. Similar records may also be found in local record offices.

Antiquarians and local historians began to collect inscriptions in the nineteenth century (a few earlier collections are also known); their work can often be found in the journals of local historical and archaeological societies (the contents of which are listed in the county volumes of Raymond's *British genealogical library guides*); many unpublished transcriptions are held by local studies and other libraries. More recently, family history societies have undertaken the systematic transcription of inscriptions in their own areas covering each churchyard or cemetery in turn. This process is still continuing. Such transcripts are often made in triplicate, so that copies can be lodged with the local society, the relevant local studies library, and the Society of Genealogists (the latter's collection is listed by Collins). Many have been published on microfiche or in book format; and are listed by Perkins or Hampson, and also in Raymond's county volumes (see p. 19).

More recently, efforts have been made to computerise the transcription of inscriptions. Many family history societies now hold databases of inscriptions; indexes to some of these are available on a pay per view basis at the *Family History Online* website. In recent years, innumerable individuals have created internet sites for the transcriptions they have made themselves. There are so many of these sites that Raymond required an entire volume to list them.

It might be added that the National Maritime Museum is collecting inscriptions relating to British seamen, shipwrights, victims of ship-wrecks, ship owners, *etc.* These are mostly pre-1914.

Websites
* Maritime Memorials: commemorating seafarers and victims of maritime disasters
  www.nmm.ac.uk/memorials/

Further Reading

- 'Monumental inscriptions', in STEEL, D.J., *et al. National index of parish registers, volume 1. Sources of births, marriages and deaths before 1837.* Society of Genealogists, 1968.
- COLLINS, L. *Monumental inscriptions in the library of the Society of Genealogists.* 2 vols. Society of Genealogists, 1984-7.
- KEMP, BRIAN. *English church monuments.* B. J. Batsford, 1980.
- RAYMOND, STUART A. *Monumental inscriptions on the web: a directory.* F.F.H.S., 2002.

Chapter 7

The Census

One of the major tasks facing the genealogist is to locate their ancestors at particular dates, and to place them in family groups. The nineteenth century census enumerators' schedules provide invaluable support in this endeavour. Any list of names has its genealogical uses; the census is the list of names *par excellence*, since it lists the names of everyone living in a particular house on a particular night, and states (from 1851) the relationship of all members of the household to its head. The fact that this information can be combined with information derived from civil registration means that, for genealogists, the nineteenth century is probably the easiest period to research.

The census has been taken every ten years since 1801, with the exception of 1941, when Britain was at war. Its aim was statistical; the bureaucrats had no idea that their work would be mulled over by millions of twenty-first century genealogists. The returns made by the earliest enumerators are consequently of little use to the genealogist, since they only provide numbers, not names. It should be noted, however, that a very few lists of names from the 1801, 1821 and 1831 censuses have survived amongst parish records, *etc.* and are listed by Gibson & Medlycott, and by Chapman. The earliest census schedules of genealogical value which cover the whole country are those for 1841. For the nineteenth century, the dates on which the census was taken were as follows:

1841	6 June
1851	30 March
1861	7 April
1871	2 April
1881	3 April
1891	5 April

From 1841, the census was administered by the Registrar General, and used the same districts that were used for civil registration. A full list of these is given by Lumas; see also chapter 3 above. Each registration district was divided into sub-districts, which in turn were divided into enumeration districts, based on civil parishes, and covering a few hundred households. An enumerator was made responsible for each district; he distributed and collected individual householder's schedules, and copied the details into his own enumerator's book. The original householder's schedules were destroyed later.

The questions asked, and the design of the enumerators' schedules, varied over time. The information given in 1841 included:

- the place, i.e. the name or location of each dwelling (with an indication of uninhabited houses)
- the "names of each person who abode therein the preceding night"
- the age and sex of each person named; ages were rounded down to the nearest five years for persons over fifteen, although this instruction was not always followed
- the "profession, trade, or employment, or of independent means". Abbreviations used here include NK=not known; FS=female servant; MS=male servant
- "where born" - but this column only states "whether born in the same county", also giving the option of stating "whether born in Scotland, Ireland or foreign parts".

In subsequent census years, rather more information was given. The additional columns in 1851 were

- "relation to head of family"
- "condition", i.e. marital status
- "whether blind or deaf and dumb"

The column for age also gave a precise age, rather than one rounded down, and the 'where born' column gave the parish and county. In 1871, the blind or deaf and dumb column also gave the options of "imbecile or idiot" and "lunatic"; in 1891 these were offered as a single option. The 1891 schedules also state whether employer, employed, or neither, and give the number of rooms in houses if over five. The Welsh returns for 1891 also had a column for language spoken, which offered as options 'Welsh', 'English', or 'both'.

The original census schedules are now held by the Family Records Centre and are not normally seen by the public. Instead, microfilm (or, for 1891, microfiche) are produced. Microfilm or microfiche of these schedules are also held by many record offices and libraries (listed by Gibson & Hampson), family history societies, *etc.* They are also increasingly being made available commercially on CD, and a project is currently in progress to make the 1891 schedules available via the internet. Fiche for particular enumeration districts can be purchased from the Reprographic Ordering department of the National Archives, who will supply details of prices if you provide a full reference for the enumeration book you require.

Numerous census indexes are also available in book format, on microfiche and CD, and on the internet. Family history societies have taken a leading role in this field, and have published many indexes. Commercial organisations and a few societies are now producing numerous indexes on CD. Published indexes and internet sites can be identified by consulting the various titles by Raymond, Perkins and Hampson listed at the end of chapter 1. A comprehensive listing of census indexes (excluding internet sites) is provided by Gibson & Hampson's *Marriage and census indexes.* Internet sites can often be located by checking the county and parish pages at **www.genuki.org.uk**. Many county indexes created by family history societies are available, on a pay per view basis, at the Family History Online site.

At present the only censuses which are comprehensively indexed are those for 1881 and 2001; the latter is outside of the scope of this book. The 1881 fiche index is widely available in libraries, record offices, and family history societies. There is also an internet version at the *Family Search* website. This index has two major advantages over most indexes. Firstly, it enables a comprehensive search to be made at the national level, if the internet is being used, or at the county level, if only the fiche is available. Secondly, the internet version includes a transcript of the original, rather than being just an index with simply names and folio numbers. It also provides the Family History Library film number, which enables the Family History Centres of the Latter Day Saints to obtain the microfilm of the original enumerator's book, and the National Archives reference which will allow you to locate the original book if you have access to a microfilm elsewhere.

There are actually three separate indexes for 1881: surname, birthplace, and census place. A separate 'as enumerated' section provides a full transcript of the original, which is particularly useful as it enables one to see at a glance the entire household of a particular ancestor, with all the census information for each individual member. The three indexes also include most of the census information for particular individuals. The birthplace index is an unusual feature for a census index, but a most useful one: it enables you to locate persons of the same name born in the same place, who may well be brothers and sisters, or perhaps other relatives. Its value is only limited by the vagaries of the original schedules, which may give only a vague place of birth, e.g. London when Paddington is meant. It should be consulted in conjunction with the name index, which may help to locate other relatives.

Census indexes are subject to the same strictures as indexes to other sources: it must be remembered that they are only indexes, and that they are subject to human error. You should always check the microfilm of the original enumerators' books when you find an index entry.

Most census indexes will give you the Family Records Centre class and piece number, together with the folio number for the particular entry. The method by which particular enumerators' books can be located does need to be understood by researchers. There is a separate class number for most census year; these are:

1841	HO 107	1871	RG 10
1851	HO 107	1881	RG 11
1861	RG 9	1891	RG 12

Within these classes, enumeration books are arranged by piece number. This number, which will include five or six books, is usually cited by indexes, which should also include a folio number to help find the particular page referred to. If there is no index, and it is desired to consult the enumeration book for a particular parish, then the census place index for the particular year should be consulted to identify the registration district and sub-district; if you are researching in an urban area you will need to consult street indexes. The information in these indexes, i.e. page numbers for 1841, registration district numbers for subsequent censuses, will enable you to turn to the appropriate entry in the census reference books to find the relevant piece number, which will enable you to find the place on the appropriate microfilm. Much more detailed guidance is given by Colwell and by Lumas.

The information found in census schedules should always be subjected to critical analysis. There is always the possibility that either the enumerator, or the householder - or both - have made errors, and included incorrect information. Entries for the same individuals in successive censuses should always be compared and contrasted. Places of birth and ages are particularly prone to vary between censuses; it should be realised that some people simply did not know when and where they were born, and guessed answers, perhaps wrongly. There is also the possibility that enumerators simply failed to locate all the residents in their areas - some may have deliberately evaded being counted.

The census schedules, in theory, record everyone who slept in a particular place on a particular evening. Consequently, they do not show entire households where one or more member was absent on that night. And they certainly do not show complete families. Teenage sons and daughters in particular are quite likely to have been living-in servants in other households. They may also have been at boarding school. Family members may have been in an institution such as a hospital, a work-house or a prison; they may have been travelling, perhaps staying at an hotel, at sea, or abroad. There are numerous reasons why they may have been absent from home on census night. Some of these can be checked, some can not. It is always worth checking census schedules covering local institutions. For 1841, the names of men aboard ship were not recorded; this was remedied in 1851, although some ships which were away from home, especially for a long period, may have been missed.

Despite these problems, the nineteenth century census enumerators' books constitute one of the most important sources for genealogical research. They can be used to identify the members of particular families at a particular time and place. They provide basic information about each individual: their name, age, residence, birthplace, occupation, and relationship to other members of their household. The clues provided by the census enable searches to be made in many of the other sources described in this book, and especially in both civil and parish registers, which may lead to much earlier information. Comparisons may be made with the information in trade directories (chapter 13), electoral registers (chapter 14), and rate lists (chapter 14). The information given under the heading 'profession, trade or employment' could be used to make a search of occupational sources (chapter 9) which may provide interesting insights into ancestral lives.

Unofficial Census Listings
It has already been noted that a few lists of names from early censuses have survived amongst parish records. There are similar lists from later censuses, and there are also many lists similar to the census compiled for a variety of other purposes, for example, visiting books compiled by parochial clergy. These 'local censuses' are listed by Gibson & Medlycott, and by Chapman.

Web Pages
- Census of England and Wales: Read this First
  **www.catalogue.nationalarchives.gov.uk/
  RdLeaflet.asp?sLeafletID=326**

- Census Returns
  **www.familyrecords.gov.uk/frc/pdfs/
  census_returns.pdf**

- England and Wales: Census
  www.genuki.org.uk/big/eng/Census.html

- Gendocs: Census Returns for England & Wales
  www.gendocs.demon.co.uk/census.html

- How to use ... the 1841 to 1891 Census Returns
  www.familyrecords.gov.uk/frc/pdfs/
  HTU_1841-1891_Census.pdf

- 1881 British Census Indexes Resource Guide
  www.familysearch.org/Eng/
  Click on 'search', 'Research Helps', 'E' (for England),
  and scroll down to title. Various other useful pages
  are also available on this site.

- 1891 Census
  www.1891-census.co.uk/

Further Reading

- LUMAS, SUE. *Making use of the census.* Public
  Record Office readers guide 1. 4th ed. 2002.
- COLWELL, STELLA. *The Family Records Centre: a
  user's guide.* 2nd ed. Public Record Office readers
  guide 17. 2002.
- GIBSON, JEREMY, & HAMPSON, ELIZABETH. *Census
  returns 1841-1891 in microform: a directory to local
  holdings in Great Britain; Channel Islands; Isle of
  Man.* 6th ed. F.F.H.S., 2001.
- GIBSON, JEREMY, & HAMPSON, ELIZABETH. *Marriage
  and census indexes for family historians.* 8th ed.
  F.F.H.S., 2000.

- HIGGS, EDWARD. *A clearer sense of the census: the Victorian censuses and historical research.* Public Record Office handbooks **28.** H.M.S.O., 1996.
- HIGGS, EDWARD. 'Census returns in England and Wales', in THOMPSON, K.M. *Short guides to records. Second series, 26-48.* Historical Association, 1997, 59-62.
- *Using census returns.* Pocket guides to family history. Public Record Office, 2000.

Unofficial Censuses

- CHAPMAN, COLIN, R. *Pre-1841 censuses and population listings in the British Isles.* 5th ed. Dursley: Lochin Publishing, 1998.
- GIBSON, J.S.W., & MEDLYCOTT, M. *Local census listings, 1522-1930: holdings in Great Britain.* 3rd ed. F.F.H.S., 2001.

Chapter 8

Wills

It is rare for the genealogist to discover personal documents written by, or at the direction of, his or her ancestors. The major exception to this rule are wills. Enormous numbers of wills have survived and may be consulted. Some of them may have been written by lawyers, or perhaps clergymen, but they all provide personal information - sometimes very detailed - about testators. And in general the information in them is likely to be more trustworthy than is the case for most other sources.

The format of wills underwent no great changes in the nineteenth century, despite the fact that jurisdiction over probate was transferred from ecclesiastical courts to a civil court in 1858. The testator would begin by stating his name, residence, and occupation. In previous centuries it had been usual to express one's faith in God when writing a will; this custom was already beginning to decline at the end of the eighteenth century, and continued to decline throughout our period. In invoking God, the testator might also make provision for his burial, and thus give an indication of where an entry in a burial register, or a monumental inscription, might be found. The main part of the will dealt with the distribution of the estate, normally including bequests to spouse and surviving children, and perhaps also to relatives, friends, and employees. An executor or executors would then be named; he or she was likely to be a relative, often the chief beneficiary. If the relationship is not stated this should be checked in other sources. The executor would be instructed to pay any debts, and to meet funeral expenses, and the testator would sign the will in the presence of witnesses who would also sign. They could not be beneficiaries of the will, but their names are worth recording.

The information to be found in a will is likely to help you to build a picture of your ancestor's life: his wealth and social status, some of his likes and dislikes, some of the goods that he owned. Not every will provides the same information; however, it is likely that you could discover at least some of the following:

- The names of his spouse, children, and grandchildren. All surviving children are likely to be named, although this is not invariable. However, children who pre-deceased their father may not be mentioned. And you should avoid the assumption that a spouse is necessarily the mother of all the children of a testator; he may have re-married.
- The surnames of any married daughters
- The names of other relatives, and relationships within the family
- Instructions may be given for burial, perhaps naming the place of interment

- The social status and / or occupation of your ancestor may be given, or may be deduced from the bequest of the tools of his trade
- Bequests of furniture, clothing, and other goods may indicate the lifestyle of the testator
- Intimate details of a person's life may emerge from wills. The testator may take the opportunity to finally acknowledge an illegitimate child. He may also pass comments on other members of the family, perhaps referring to his 'loving wife', or denying a wastrel son more than a minimal bequest.

The interpretation of a will is not necessarily straightforward. It must be borne in mind that a will was merely a part of the process of inheritance. A son who received a token bequest of a shilling may have already received a substantial part of his father's estate. A spouse for whom no provision is made in a will may have already been provided for. A married daughter may have had property settled on her at her marriage. Landed property may not be mentioned in a will at all, its descent having already been dealt with. Until 1858, the probate courts had no jurisdiction over the descent of real property; any dispute had to be settled in the Court of Chancery or one of the other crown courts.

Who made wills? Most testators were men. Until the passing of the Married Women's Property Act in 1882, the property of married women was deemed to belong to their husbands, and they could only make wills with their husbands' permission. However, there are many wills of widows and spinsters. The greater proportion of wills were made by the middle and upper classes, who needed to make provision for the distribution of their goods. Most labourers did not own sufficient possessions to render a will necessary. Nevertheless, some members of the lower classes did make wills, and it is always worth checking whether this was the case.

Pre-1858 Wills

Until 1858, wills were subject to the jurisdiction of a wide range of (mainly) ecclesiastical courts. Probate was granted by officials of these courts, and the wills themselves (or copies of them) were stored as court records. It is therefore necessary to understand the structure of ecclesiastical courts in order to locate wills for particular individuals.

Archdeaconry courts stood at the bottom of the hierarchy. If a man's property lay wholly within one archdeaconry, his executors would apply to the official principal of that court for grant of probate. If, however, he owned property to the value of £5 or more (£10 in London) in a different archdeaconry, then jurisdiction lay with a diocesan court. And if his goods were in different dioceses, then jurisdiction lay with the Prerogative Court of either Canterbury or York (P.C.C. or P.C.Y.). There were also many 'peculiars', i.e. areas where normal ecclesiastical jurisdiction did not apply; for example, Uffculme in

Devon was held by a prebendary of Salisbury Cathedral, who conducted his own prebendal court. Not all peculiars were ecclesiastical; some were held by the crown, by manorial lords, and by boroughs, although by 1800 many were moribund.

In practice, executors could choose to apply for grant of probate to a number of different courts. They frequently chose a superior court, often, but not always, for reasons of social prestige. The proportion of grants of probate made in P.C.C. rose in the nineteenth century, partly because of the prestige factor, but also because the Bank of England, which administered government stock (gilts) held by many testators, decided in 1812 to refuse recognition to grants of probate made by any other court. The decreasing value of money also meant that an ever increasing proportion of testators were coming within the jurisdiction of the P.C.C.; inflation was continually eroding the value of the £5 threshold.

The records of P.C.C. are held by the National Archives, who have now digitised all their court copies of wills (PROB 11) and made them available on the internet at the *Documents Online* site. The word 'copies' needs emphasis; these are not the original wills, but copies transcribed by clerks into the court's records.

Also available online is an index to Bank of England will extracts for 1717 to 1845. These relate to testators who possessed money in public funds administered by the Bank. The extracts were intended to be used by the Bank to enable them to transfer such funds into the ownership of heirs; they are not, therefore, complete wills, but only extracts, although they do indicate in which court a will was proved - which, after 1812, will have been the P.C.C.

Most other surviving pre-1858 wills are to be found in county record offices, although those for P.C.Y. are in the Borthwick Institute of Historical Research. There are published indexes to the majority of collections, although unfortunately, some of then end in 1800. The British Record Society's *Index Library* series, which is widely available in public and university libraries, has the aim of publishing indexes to all pre-1858 wills, and some volumes covering the nineteenth century are available. The county volumes of Raymond's *British genealogical library guides* series include lists of all published indexes. A full listing of probate courts, giving the location of their records, and brief details of both published and unpublished indexes, is provided by Gibson and Churchill. Pre-1858 wills may also be located by consulting the Death Duty registers, discussed below.

Post-1858 Wills
The Probate Act 1857 transferred all probate jurisdictions to a new civil Court of Probate, with effect from 12 January 1858. This court was merged into the Probate, Divorce and Admiralty Divisions of the High Court in 1875, which in its turn became the Family Division in 1970. Applications for grant of

probate had to be made to the court's Principal Probate Registry, or to one of its many district probate registries and sub-registries.

If a grant of probate was made in a district registry, that office will have kept the original will, made a copy for its own register, and sent a copy to the Principal Probate Registry. The latter (now known as the Probate Registry) therefore holds copies of all wills proved since 1858. An annual *National probate calendar,* which is now widely available not only in district registries, but also in record offices, local studies libraries, family history societies, *etc.,* provides a detailed index. It notes the deceased's name, date of death, when and where the will was proved, the names of executors or administrators, and the value of the estate. Sometimes the occupations of both testators and executors are given. Until 1892 the addresses of executors and administrators were also given, as was their relationship to the deceased. Hence this *calendar* alone is a useful source of information. It should be noted, however, that the copy held by the Principal Registry has hand-written additions which are not present on other copies; this includes the folio numbers of London registered wills, which are required for ordering copies. You should also bear in mind that the indexes list wills proved in a particular year; they do not relate to the date of death. It may be many years after a death before a will is proved; consequently, some wills from the early part of the century will be found in the Principal Registry, rather than in the ecclesiastical courts.

With the information provided by the *calendar,* you can apply to either see the will, or to obtain a copy. This is almost always worth doing; it will be a useful check on the information provided by the calendar, and is likely to yield much more information. If, however, the *calendar* defines the executor or administrator as the 'universal legatee', this means that the testator left all his possessions to one person, and the will is likely to reveal little extra information. Wills can be inspected in the Principal Registry, and in district registries (or in record offices if the records have been transferred). There is a fee for inspection, and for copying. If you wish to order a copy by post, you should contact the York office at the address below, giving the date of death. Details of the whereabouts of district registry copies of wills are given by Gibson and Churchill, and also by McLaughlin. The district registries are not able to provide copies by post, although record offices may be able to do so.

Other Probate Documents

Wills are not the only documents generated by the process of probate. The grant of probate is also worth checking; it may add detail to the Principal Registry's *calendar.* For pre-1858 wills it is often written on the back of the will. If there was no will, then letters of administration would have been required. They would also have been required if no executor was named, or if the executor was unwilling or unable to act, e.g. if he was a minor. These letters are indexed in the *calendar,* but contain much less information than wills. They will specify the deceased's name, address, occupation, and the date and place of death. The name, address, and occupation of the administrator will be recorded, as will his or her relationship to the deceased. The value of the estate will also be given.

Probate inventories may occasionally be found, although these are much less common than in earlier centuries. They specify the decedent's name, parish, and perhaps his occupation or status; they list and value all his goods, giving the names of the appraisers, and the date on which the inventory was made. They may incidentally include other names, e.g. debtors. Inventories, where they are available, are invaluable sources for examining the life-styles of ancestors.

Probate disputes may also yield documentation; prior to 1858 these could have been heard in ecclesiastical courts - especially the P.C.C. - or in the Court of Chancery; subsequently they were dealt with in the Court of Probate. The records of the P.C.C. are described by Scott, and also by Grannum & Taylor.

Addresses
Principal Registry of the Family Division
First Avenue House
42-49, High Holborn
London, WCIV 6NP

The Postal Searches and Copies Department
The Probate Registry
1st Floor, Castle Chambers
Clifford Street
York, YO1 9RG

Death Duty Registers

Death duties were introduced in 1796. The scope of this tax was relatively narrow at first, but was gradually extended during the course of the nineteenth century; by mid-century, most of those who left wills were liable to be at least recorded in the registers.

These registers, compiled by the Estate Duty Office, are now in the National Archives (IR 26); indexes are in IR 27. They run from 1796 to 1903 (although some from the 1890's have been destroyed), and are based on extracts from wills and administrations. Consequently, they may be useful in locating original probate records. They often provide much additional information, and could be annotated many years after they were first compiled. They show not only the actual value of an estate (as opposed to the value stated in probate records), but also what happened to it after probate - which can usefully be compared with the provisions of the will. The will extracts give the name, address and occupation of the deceased; the dates of the will and grant of probate, names, addresses and occupations of the executors or administrators, and details of legacies, trustees, annuities, *etc.*. The duty paid is noted, as is much information concerning beneficiaries and next of kin. Bequests to certain relations were exempt in the early periods of the tax, and consequently relationships are noted, as are the marriages and deaths of widows and other beneficiaries, births of posthumous children and grandchildren, changes of address, *etc.; etc.*

These registers are available on microfilm at the National Archives and the Family Records Centre until 1858; after that date three days notice is required to consult the originals at the National Archives. Indexes to them for 1796 to 1903 (IR 27) are available on microfilm at the Family Records Centre (and also, to 1858, at the Society of Genealogists). Further details of these records and their indexes may be found on the web sites listed below. Unfortunately, most of the copy wills held by the Estate Duty Office have been destroyed; however, some for Devon, Cornwall and Somerset were sent to the respective record offices to make up for the loss of their other probate records during the blitz of Exeter.

Web Pages

- Probate Records
  www.catalogue.nationalarchives.gov.uk/
  RdLeaflet.asp?sLeafletID=168

- Wills before 1858: Where to Start
  www.catalogue.nationalarchives.gov.uk/
  RdLeaflet.asp?sLeaflet/ID=220

- Wills and Death Duty Registers
  **www.nationalarchives.gov.uk/pathways/
  familyhistory/gallery1/wills.htm**

- Wills and Death Duty Records after 1858
  **www.catalogue.nationalarchives.gov.uk/
  RdLeaflet.asp?sLeafletID=219**

- Documents Online: About the Wills
  **www.documentsonline.nationalarchives.gov.uk/
  wills.asp**

  Details of P.C.C. wills online

- Probate Records and Family History
  www.courtservice.gov.uk/cms/3800.htm
  Details from the Principal Registry

- Bank of England Will Extracts Index 1717-1845
  **www.originsnetwork.com/help/
  popup-aboutbo-boe2.htm**

Death Duties
- Death Duty Records from 1796 (Domestic records
  information 57
  **www.catalogue.nationalarchives.gov.uk/
  RdLeaflet.asp?sLeafletID=107**

- How to interpret Death Duty Registers
  **www.nationalarchives.gov.uk/
  RdLeaflet.asp?sLeafletID=245**

- How to Interpret Death Duty Records
  www.familyrecords.gov.uk/frc/pdfs/
  death_duty_interpretation.pdf

- About the Index to Death Duty Registers 1796-1903
  www.nationalarchivist.com/index02/about.cfm
  The index itself is still forthcoming

- How to Interpret Death Duty Registers
  www.nationalarchives.gov.uk/
  RdLeaflet.asp?sLeafletID=245

Further Reading

- COX, JANE. *Affection defying the power of death: wills, probate, & death duty records.* An introduction to ... series. F.F.H.S., 1993.
- COLLINS, AUDREY. *Using wills after 1858, and First Avenue House.* Basic facts about ... series. F.F.H.S., 1998.
- GIBSON, JEREMY, & CHURCHILL, ELSE. *Probate jurisdictions: where to look for wills.* 5th ed. F.F.H.S., 2002.
- GRANNUM, KAREN, & TAYLOR, NIGEL. *Wills and other probate records: a practical guide to researching your ancestor's last documents.* National Archives, 2004.
- McLAUGHLIN, EVE. *Modern wills from 1858.* 6th ed. Haddenham: Varneys Press, 2001.
- McLAUGHLIN, EVE. *Wills before 1858.* 6th ed. Haddenham: Varneys Press, 2002.

- SCOTT, MIRIAM. *Prerogative Court of Canterbury: wills and other probate records.* Public Record Office readers guide 15. 1997.
- *Using wills.* Pocket guides to family history. Public Record Office, 2000.

Chapter 9

Earning A Living

It has already been argued that family history is more than the bare bones of pedigrees. Those pedigrees need to be placed in the context of the society in which the people named on them lived and worked. 'Worked' is the key word in this chapter. If we wish to understand how our ancestors lived, we must study how they worked, we must seek information on their occupations. Work was a major part of our ancestors' lives, and occupational records can provide the family historian with invaluable information. Fortunately, the records of employment are extensive, although much has been destroyed, and it may sometimes be difficult to trace and use them.

Many of the sources that are discussed elsewhere in this book - the census, birth marriage and death certificates, trade directories, *etc.* - are likely to provide basic information on ancestral trades and professions. The nature of particular trades mentioned in these sources may not always be evident, and it may be useful to check one of the dictionaries of occupations listed below for elucidation.

If you are able to identify an ancestor's occupation, then it may be possible to check for further information in occupational sources. In order to do this, the easiest first step is to consult the present author's *Occupational sources for genealogists,* or one of its local companion volumes, e.g. *Londoner's occupations,* in order to see whether any detailed information relating to that occupation has been published. It may also be useful to consult the listing of occupational websites in Raymond's *Family history on the web.* (3rd ed. F.F.H.S., 2004).

Books and web-sites on occupations tend to fall into several distinct categories: guides to sources written specifically for genealogists; archival guides; lists of men and women in specific occupations; biographical dictionaries; histories of particular occupations.

Guides written specifically for genealogists are particularly useful, since they provide expert guidance through the maze of records. Books such as Shearman's *My ancestor was a policeman* Richards' *Was your grandfather a railwayman?* and Pappalardo's *Tracing your naval ancestors* provide essential information for all who are seeking ancestors in those occupations. There are many similar works covering occupations as diverse as merchant seamen and gasmen, publicans and soldiers, convicts and coalminers, too many to be listed here. Many web pages provide a similar service: coastguards, apothecaries, and teachers are just a few of the occupations for which research guidance is available on the internet. Both books and websites may be identified in the works by Raymond mentioned above (although many new guides have been written since *Occupational sources* was published).

   A more general work written by E.D.Probert with the genealogist in mind deals with *Company and business records for family historians* and includes information on topics such as personnel records and registers of directors. There are also many archival guides not written specifically for genealogists, which may nevertheless be useful to the family historian. Probert's book, for example, may be complemented by Armstrong & Jones's *Business documents* and by several other works on business and company records. Guides to the archives of specific industries may yield much valuable information; for example, there is a chapter on staff records in C.J.Edwards *Railway records: a guide to sources.* (Public Record Office, 2001). The archives of some 1,200 firms are briefly described and located in the Historical Manuscripts Commission's *Records of British business and industry, 1760-1914: textiles and leather.* (H.M.S.O., 1990). On the internet, the Hospital Records Database (**www.nationalarchives.gov.uk/hospitalrecords**) and the University of Bristol Theatre Collections (**www.bris.ac.uk/theatrecollection**) list extensive collections of archives which are likely to lead to much information on health professionals, and theatrical workers respectively. There are many similar sites.

   Archival guides may sometimes be useful simply as lists of names. That is the case with

Pappalardo's *Royal Navy lieutenants' passing certificates 1691-1902*. On the internet similar information is provided by the Black Sheep Index **www.lightage.demon.co.uk/BSI/NOTES.htm** which indexes the names of 120,000 villains, 1810-1900. Lists of names of people in specific occupations have frequently been published. Professional organizations published lists of members, sometimes in order to comply with governmental requirements. *The register of Veterinary Surgeons,* for example, was first published by the Royal College of Veterinary Surgeons in 1858, and was re-issued irregularly (annually from 1884) in accordance with an act of parliament. Similarly, the General Medical Council has issued *The Medical register* annually since 1859. Lists of members were published in the nineteenth century for organizations as diverse as the Library Association, the Royal Institute of British Architects, and the Society of Accountants and Auditors.

Similar works were also published commercially. *Crockfords clerical directory* began to list all Church of England clergy in 1858. The *Law list* is a title applied to a number of different publications issued by various publishers throughout the century which listed judges, barristers, solicitors and other members of the legal profession. Similarly, there were numerous different *Army lists* issued by various publishers. These lists would not have been regarded as 'trade' directories at the time, but they performed similar functions to works such as E.G.Easton's *The*

Metropolitan dairyman's directory and handbook of reference (Cowkeeper and Dairyman's journal, 1886) and *The Post Office directory of the cabinet, furniture and upholstery trades.* (12 issues, Kelly & Co., 1877-1936).

Works such as these were intended for use by contemporaries, and their value for historical study was not recognised at the time they were published. Biographical dictionaries, by contrast, were intended to provide a historical record, even though some were issued in the life-time of their subjects. Numerous biographical dictionaries relating to particular trades and professions are available; they usually include details of parentage, date and place of birth; sometimes more genealogical information may be given. They provide brief biographies of their subjects, emphasising their contribution to the particular trade or profession. Good examples include G.Beard & C.Gilbert's *Dictionary of English furniture makers 1660-1840* (Furniture History Society, 1986) and J.M.Bellamy & J.Saville's *Dictionary of labour biography* (8 vols; Macmillan, 1972-86).

Histories of particular industries, professions, trades, *etc.,* may also yield useful information. Sometimes such works include lists of names; for example, D.E.Allen's *The botanists: a history of the Botanical Society of the British Isles through a hundred and fifty years.* (St. Paul's Bibliographies, 1986) includes a full list of society members.

Where such histories include detailed references,

their bibliographies may provide useful leads to potential sources of information for family history; such is the case, for example, with Hanson's *The canal boatmen 1760-1914* (Manchester University Press, 1975).

If you know the name of a firm for which an ancestor worked, it may be worth checking to see whether a history of that firm has been published. The bibliographies of Goodall and Zarach provide comprehensive listings of business histories.

Once you have checked the published sources, you may find it useful to check whether any original sources survive; indeed, the books and web sites mentioned above may provide some indication of what is available. Archives relating to occupations fall into three main categories: staff records of employers, the archives of professional and trade organizations, and administrative records created by regulatory agencies of government.

The personnel records of employers may contain much valuable information - although equally, they may have been lost or destroyed. Those records which do survive may take some tracking down. The A2A index and Archives Hub (see pp. 17-18) are both worth checking for information on collections and locations. Some firms may still hold their own archives; a handful, e.g. the Post Office, have their own dedicated archive repositories. The National Archives holds personnel records from most government departments, including the armed forces (which are extensive); it also holds some of the archives of the various nationalised transport companies, including some of their predecessor companies such as the Great Western Railway. County record offices hold the records of many, but far from all, businesses which operated in their locality. They also hold personnel records relating to staff employed by their own local government authority and its predecessors.

Personnel records may be difficult to locate, but the information to be found in them may provide a great deal of information. Applications for jobs, records of appointments and service, apprenticeship records, establishment registers, pension records, staff magazines, *etc., etc.,* may all include important evidence for family history.

Job applications and testimonials may be particularly useful; they are likely to provide details of age, address, education, qualifications, previous employers, names of referees, *etc., etc.* and may suggest other sources which could be checked. The 'entry papers' 1820-70 for excise officers, held in the National Archives at CUST 116, provide an example of what may be found; they are letters of recommendation, setting out age, birthplace, marital status, and a character reference for each applicant, as well as a statement of each officer's proficiency in writing, spelling and arithmetic.

Staff magazines are another potential source of information, since they often recorded appointments, promotions, transfers and retirements, *etc.*, and also included obituaries. Similar information may also be found in trade journals. The *Great Western Railway magazine*, for example was published from 1862 to 1864 and 1888 onwards, and included an increasing amount of staff information.

Professional and trade organizations also hold useful records; their membership registers and records should enable you to trace their members' entire careers. Entry to many professions was by examination, and the records of results obtained are often still in the archives. For example, the archives of the Institute of Chartered Accountants, held by London's Guildhall Library, include membership records from 1880, and examination records from 1882.

Membership registers were frequently published and have already been discussed. The membership records of trade unions also contain much information; these are discussed in chapter 11.

It has already been seen in other contexts how the nineteenth-century 'age of reform' promoted the compilation of records such as the census and civil registration, which are vital for genealogical research. The impetus of reform was also experienced by certain occupations in which government took a particular interest. Concern for the nation's health, for example, led to the regulation of the medical profession, and to the requirement that the names of all doctors be published annually in the *Medical register*. Defence requirements led to the registration of all merchant seamen between 1835 and 1857; the resultant registers, now in various BT classes in the National Archives, are the first place to check for ordinary seamen in that period. At the local level, Quarter Sessions and local councils continued to licence various trades, such as victuallers and innkeepers, pedlars and hawkers, printers and gamekeepers; licence registers may be found in county record offices.

Soldiers

It is probable that a greater proportion of our ancestors served in the army during the nineteenth century than were employed in any other occupation. It is relatively easy to trace the careers of officers, whose names should be included in the *Army lists* which were regularly published throughout the century, and which are widely available in reference libraries. These lists record the regiment in which an officer served, information which is essential if army records are to be further searched, since the War Office papers in the National Archives are arranged by regiment. A wide range of records are available. Service records (WO 25, 54 & 76) may include details of family and birthplace; the Commander in Chief memoranda papers (WO 31) give details of appointments, promotions and resignations (to 1870); half pay ledgers and lists in various PMG classes record who was being paid, and where they lived; widows and dependants may be traced in files related to various pensions for them (in PMG 9-11 & WO 23-5).

If your ancestor served in 'other ranks', you may need to discover his regiment before you can trace army records. Some of the sources already discussed, e.g. marriage certificates, the census, may provide this information. Each stage in a soldier's career should have been recorded. Attestation papers and description books were written on joining up; muster books and regimental pay lists record the presence of soldiers in particular regiments; casualty returns and discharge papers marked either death or discharge; the records of Chelsea and Kilmainham Hospitals record pensioners. These records are found in a wide variety of classes in the National Archives.

Army records are extensive, and cannot be described in detail here; many sources have not even been mentioned. The most up to date source of guidance are the many pages dealing with the army on the National Archives web site; the books by Fowler & Spencer, and by the Watts, should also be consulted, as should the relevant chapters of Bevan's *Tracing your ancestors in the Public Record Office*. (6th ed. Public Record Office, 2002).

Further Reading
A. General Bibliographies
- RAYMOND, STUART A. *Occupational sources for genealogists.* 2nd ed. F.F.H.S., 1996.

- RAYMOND, STUART A. *Londoner's occupations: a genealogical guide.* 2nd ed. F.F.H.S., 2001. Further volumes cover Surrey/Sussex and Yorkshire. There are also sections listing works on occupations in most of Raymond's county bibliographies.

B. Lists of occupations
- CULLING, JOYCE. *An introduction to occupations: a preliminary list.* 2nd ed. F.F.H.S., 1999.
- TWINING, ANDREW, & TWINING, SANDRA. *Dictionary of old trades and occupations.* Kogarah, N.S.W.: Twinings Secretarial, 1993.
- WATERS, C. *A dictionary of old trades, titles and occupations.* Rev. ed. Countryside Books, 2002.

C. Company Records and Histories
- PROBERT, E.D. *Company and business records for family historians.* F.F.H.S., 1994.
- ARMSTRONG, J., & JONES, S. *Business documents.* Mansell, 1987.
- GOODALL, FRANCIS. *A bibliography of British business histories.* Aldershot: Gower, 1987.
- ZARACH, STEPHANIE. *Debretts bibliography of British business history.* Macmillan, 1986.

D. Some Guides to Specific Occupations
Brewers, Publicans & Victuallers
- GIBSON, JEREMY, & HUNTER, JUDITH. *Victuallers licences: records for family and local historians.* 2nd ed. F.F.H.S., 1997.

- FOWLER, SIMON. *Researching brewery and publican ancestors.* F.F.H.S., 2003.

Coalminers
- TONKS, DAVID. *My ancestor was a coalminer.* Society of Genealogists Enterprises, 2003.

Merchant Seamen
- WATTS, CHRISTOPHER T., & WATTS, MICHAEL J. *My ancestor was a merchant seaman.* 2nd ed. Society of Genealogists, 2002.

Policemen
- SHEARMAN, ANTONY. *My ancestor was a policeman.* Society of Genealogists, 2000.

Railwaymen
- RICHARDS, TOM. *Was your grandfather a railwayman?* 4th ed. F.F.H.S., 2002.

Seamen
- PAPPALARDO, BRUNO. *Tracing your naval ancestors.* Readers guide **24.** Public Record Office, 2003.
- PAPPALARDO, BRUNO. *Royal Navy lieutenants' passing certificates 1691-1902.* 2 pts. List & Index Society **289.** 2001.

Soldiers
- FOWLER, SIMON, & SPENCER, WILLIAM. *Army records for family historians.* Public Record Office readers guide **2.** 2nd ed. 1998.
- WATTS, MICHAEL, & WATTS, CHRISTOPHER J. *My ancestor was in the British Army.* Society of Genealogists, 1992.

Chapter 10

The Militia & Yeomanry

At the opening of the nineteenth century, the United Kingdom was battling the power of the Napoleonic Empire. Some of the men who served at home in that war were militia men, recruited locally for county militia regiments, which had been created in 1757. Some militia men were volunteers, but conscription was necessary to recruit the number of men needed. Each parish was obliged to find a certain number of men to serve, drawn by ballot. This required the drawing up of lists of those qualified to serve, i.e. all able bodied men aged 18 to 45. Clergy, teachers, magistrates, peers and apprentices were exempted, as were the infirm; however, all their names were included on the militia ballot lists drawn-up for the ballots. These lists, where they survive, are effectively censuses of adult males, particularly useful in view of the fact that the earliest full census to survive is usually that for 1841. They usually record occupations and any infirmities; from 1802 they record the number of children each man had; from 1806 they note men's ages. Previous service in the militia, or in the Yeomanry (see below) may also be noted. Conscription ceased in 1831, although volunteers continued to serve.

Survival of lists is patchy; they are generally found amongst the records of the Lord Lieutenants or Quarter Sessions, in county record offices. Gibson and Medlycott provide a detailed listing.

The imminent threat of French invasion in 1798 and 1803-4 forced the government to take further steps to organise local defence. One result was the drawing up of the *posse comitatus* lists of 1798, and the *levee en masse* lists of 1803. The purpose of these lists was to provide, as far as possible, for the evacuation of the civil population, the removal of cattle and produce from the path of the invader, the support of the armed forces, *etc.* They record the names and occupations of all men who were not already engaged in some military capacity. The 1803 lists in particular would have amounted to a full census if all the information required were actually given, and had more than a scatter of records survived. Where they are available (listed by Gibson & Medlycott) they list all men aged 17 to 55, including names, occupations, infirmities, marital status, number of children, and sometimes ages. They also list all householders, all non-combatants, various tradesmen such as millers and bakers, *etc., etc.* A typical example has been edited by Hoskins.

Those men who were selected by ballot had to either find a substitute, or serve with county militia regiment for five years. In peace-time, they lived at home, but spent a few weeks at training camp each year. During the Napoleonic Wars, however, they were embodied on permanent duty, usually in a county other than the one in which they were raised. Hence marriage entries in parish register may record grooms in the Militia many miles from home. When regiments were embodied, muster rolls were compiled; these are held by the National Archives (WO 13). They may also have been preserved locally in county record offices. A variety of other records held in the National Archives are identified by Spencer.

After 1831, the Militia were a voluntary force. A variety of other auxiliary troops were also raised during the French revolutionary wars; the Yeomanry (cavalry) continued in existence throughout the century, and were often used in curbing local disorder; they were responsible for the notorious 'Peterloo massacre' of 1819. Spencer lists their records. Records of militia officers are often found amongst the records of the regular army.

Web Page
• Militia 1757-1914
**www.catalogue.nationalarchives.gov.uk/
RdLeaflet.asp?sLeafletID=26**

Further Reading
• GIBSON, JEREMY, & MEDLYCOTT, MERVYN. *Militia lists and musters, 1757-1876: a directory of holdings in the British Isles.* 4th ed. F.F.H.S., 2000.
• SPENCER, WILLIAM. *Records of the Militia and Volunteer forces from 1757.* Public Record Office readers guide 3. 1993.
• HOSKINS, W.G. ed. *Exeter Militia list.* Phillimore & Co., 1972.

Chapter 11

Records of the Poor Law and the Working Classes

The late eighteenth and early nineteenth centuries were a time of rapid population growth, which led to increasing demands being placed on the old poor law system, ultimately leading to the New Poor Law Act of 1834. The idea that the community should support the poor had very long roots in England; however, pockets were not quite as long as was necessary, and accordingly the 1834 act aimed to reduce the demand on rate-payers' purses. Its prime concern was to attack the supposed 'culture of dependency' amongst the working classes, and to ensure that adult males who became unemployed were not treated as well as those who were employed on the lowest wages. This principle of 'less eligibility' led to insistence on the requirement that relief be given only to those prepared to enter the workhouse with its spartan regime and prison-like conditions. It worked. Adult able-bodied males rarely constituted more than 20% of the total workhouse population. An institution that was designed for the supposedly shiftless, improvident unemployed, in practice housed the sick, women, and children. The needs of the latter were ill-considered by the reformers of 1834, but the family historian is far more likely to find those least able to provide for themselves in poor law records than to find fit males. In one respect, however, the policy did not work. The aim to reduce out-door relief for the unemployed to nil never reached its target. Between 1859 and 1874 over 70% of adult male paupers were in receipt of out-door relief rather than resident in the workhouse. Overall, however, the 1834 legislation achieved its prime aim: to give the working class a fear and loathing of the workhouse regime, so that only those in dire necessity would accept its embrace.

One consequence of the introduction of the new poor law was the growth of friendly societies through which the working classes tried to provide insurance for themselves. Trade unions also involved themselves in similar activities - burial clubs, unemployment insurance, sickness benefits, *etc.* Genealogical authors place much more emphasis on the importance of poor law records than on friendly society and trade union records. That is due to the fact that more poor law records survive. Nevertheless, more people were involved in friendly society activity than sought to claim relief from the poor law authorities. It has been calculated that between a third and a quarter of adult males were members of friendly societies in 1872 - far more than were seeking poor relief at that time. Ancestors are more likely to have been recorded by friendly societies than by officials of the poor law. Nevertheless, the survival rate of poor law records has been much greater; also, the information they contain for each person mentioned is sometimes much more detailed.

The major administrative change introduced by the 1834 act was to transfer responsibility for poor law administration from the parish to unions of parishes. Consequently, prior to 1834 poor law records will be found with parish records; from that date the Unions kept their own records. Some records may also be found with quarter sessions records, as disputes about settlement occupied much of the time of the local bench. Some post-1834 records may also be found in the National Archives. It is difficult to use these to identify individual paupers, although they may be useful for workhouse staff. Sokoll's edition of paupers' letters from Essex includes many from the National Archives, and illustrates what can be found.

One of the first questions that was asked of applicants for poor relief, both before and after 1834, was to name their place of settlement. Settlement was a fundamental concept, since the law expected paupers to be supported from a rate assessed upon their neighbours. The relief of paupers was primarily a local concern, to be paid for from a parish rate, not a national tax. Accordingly, paupers had to be examined as to their settlement, and sent to the appropriate parish or union to obtain relief. Alternatively, the cost of relief could be re-claimed by the relieving authority from the parish which had legal responsibility.

The law of settlement was exceedingly complex, and the practices relating to it adopted by parishes and unions were very varied, and often litigious. Broadly, a person could gain legal settlement in a number of ways: by birth, by working in the parish for a full year, by holding parish office or paying parish rates, or by owning or renting property. A wife took her husband's settlement on marriage. The latest qualifying act determined the parish of settlement. This paragraph summarises a subject on which entire books were written and which many who were called upon to administer it did not understand. Disputes between different poor law authorities as to their respective responsibilities could be very expensive for rate payers.

From the genealogist's point of view, however, the consequence was a rich stream of documentation, much of which has survived. In particular, settlement examinations are amongst the most useful documents that can be found for working class biography. Applicants for relief were grilled in detail about where they had lived, and how they had earned their living, in order that the examining magistrate could determine legal settlement. The resultant examinations usually give place of birth, details of any apprenticeship, employment history with names of employers, parishes of residence, details of any properties owned or rented, and details of the pauper's wife and children (although not necessarily adult children). Other people, such as relatives or previous employers, might also be called on to give evidence.

Settlement examinations are likely to be found with removal orders. The latter often give very specific information on the pauper concerned, sometimes more than is revealed in census returns. All dependent children are usually mentioned; details of husbands in prison or transported may be given. Removal orders were not necessarily followed by actual removal; there may have been delays due to illness or confinement; the pauper may have died; the parish of settlement may have agreed to pay maintainance in or to the parish of residence. These eventualities may be noted on the reverse of the order.

Bastardy was another major issue for overseers of the poor, since the cost of lying-in and maintainance fell on the parish if no father came forward. Mothers of illegitimate children who had no means of support were questioned under oath by overseers or churchwardens as to paternity; the examination would be recorded. The father would then be required to enter into a bastardy bond or indemnity bond to pay maintainance; these bonds may be found amongst parish records. If the putative father refused to enter a bond, then he might be summoned to appear before the magistrates, and a maintainance or filiation order might be issued, which would be recorded in quarter sessions or petty sessions records. From 1844, the mother of an illegitimate child could herself apply to the justices for a maintainance order against the father; such cases are recorded in petty sessions records. Sources for bastards are discussed in detail by Paley.

Illegitimate children, orphans, and other pauper children were often apprenticed by parish or union; indentures and registers often survive amongst their records. Parishioners could be compelled to accept pauper apprentices, who might be 'bound' to learn husbandry or housewifery from a very early age. Effectively, they became unpaid menial servants. Many pauper children were sent from southern England to work as apprentices in the 'dark satanic mills' of the north. Parish apprenticeship continued until the beginning of the twentieth century, although compulsory bindings ceased to be legal after 1844.

The costs involved in administering the poor law prior to 1834 were recorded in overseers' accounts. The accounts were frequently very detailed, recording payments made directly to paupers, as well as payments for clothing, food, medical attendance, travel expenses, *etc., etc.* The paupers concerned were usually named.

These costs were paid for from the poor rate, levied on the property owners of the parish. These rates may be recorded in either the overseers or the churchwardens accounts; they provide annual listings of the ratepayers in each parish - effectively a census of heads of household, which are particularly useful in the pre-census era.

Vestry minutes may also be consulted to trace

paupers. The vestry was the governing body in parochial administration, and many poor law issues came before it. Matters such as the binding of apprentices, disputes with other parishes over questions of settlement, how particular paupers should be relieved, *etc.,* were all considered, and decisions recorded in vestry minutes.

Many of the sources described above can be found with both parish and poor law union records. An extraordinarily wide range of documents can be found amongst union records, so much so that Gibson and Rogers take several pages to list them (although few union archives now retain examples of all types). The minutes of boards of guardians contain much general information, sometimes including lists of inmates. Admission and discharge books record names, dates, occupations, ages, religion, parish, *etc.* Indoor relief lists were compiled from these books at six monthly intervals. There might be creed registers (from 1876) punishment books, leave of absence books, medical examination books, registers of clothing, *etc. etc.* For those paupers who did not enter the workhouse, relief order books, various registers of children (e.g. children boarded out, apprenticed, under the care of the guardians), returns of pauper lunatics, and a variety of other sources might be found. Workhouses also maintained their own baptism and burial registers.

The records of the poor law provide much information on family relationships, and on migration between parishes, which is not available elsewhere.

The provide an insight into the trials and tribulations of working class life, dealing with matters such as unemployment, illegitimacy, desertion, illness and bereavement. The more substantial inhabitants of a parish or union may also appear in the records, as rate-payers, overseers, guardians, magistrates, medical personnel, *etc.*

Friendly Societies

Mention has already been made of the importance of friendly societies in nineteenth-century society, and the fact that more people were involved in them than ever claimed relief under the poor law. At the beginning of the century, most of these societies were either local or for members of a particular trade. Many of these came together into the affiliated societies or 'orders' to form national societies with branches in most parts of the country; this was the origin of societies such as the Ancient Order of Foresters, the Independent Order of Oddfellows, the Independent Order of Rechabites, (etc.) These societies tended to be run by those who benefitted from their activities and played an important role in social life; however, some local and county societies were established and run by local gentry and clergy, who took a much more utilitarian approach to their duties.

The *raison d'etre* of the friendly society was the financial support of their members in illness and death. Documentation of their activities was therefore essential. Friendly society rule books may be found in quantity in both the National Archives and county record offices; however, they have little direct value for genealogists. Membership lists are much more useful; they are likely to provide names, addresses, occupations and ages; they may also give dates of death or other reasons for withdrawal. Minute books and accounts may also yield information. The major societies regularly issued directories and journals. The *Oddfellows directory,* for example, published annually from 1841, included lists of officers and directors, and details of Oddfellow lodges, i.e. branches, nation-wide. Its companion *Oddfellows magazine* reported on activities nation-wide, and included many obituaries and memoirs of leading or long-standing members.

Unfortunately, survival of these records appears to have been very patchy. However, it is worth checking the holdings of local record offices. Some are listed on the databases of the National Register of Archives and on A2A (see page 18). Logan provides a useful *Introduction to friendly society records.* The Friendly Societies Research Group website includes a number of articles offering useful guidance.

Trade Unions

Trade unions also played a role in social insurance; they sometimes offered unemployment benefits as well as burial clubs and insurance against ill-health. Members may have found that these benefits could be of more value than their bargaining power in trade disputes.

The records of unions include minutes of meetings (perhaps noting new members), membership registers, records of benefits paid, subscription records, journals, *etc., etc.* Names are most likely to be found in branch records, and it is possible to trace a member's movements around the country from them. For a detailed introduction, the guide by Southall, *et al* should be consulted.

Again, many records have been lost; however, a good collection is held at the Modern Records Centre at Warwick University: this is fully listed on its website, which also offers guidance in tracing the members of over 20 unions. Many records have also been deposited in local record offices. The Amalgamated Engineering Union has recently deposited extensive membership records, dating back to 1850, with the Society of Genealogists.

Web Pages
Poor Law
- Poor Relief
  www.devon.gov.uk/index/community/the__county/
      record__office/family__history__3/poor__relief/

- Poor Law Records 1834-1871
  www.catalogue.nationalarchives.gov.uk/
                      RdLeaflet.asp?sLeafletID=116
  Describes records of the national Poor Law Commission and Poor Law Board

- The Workhouse
  www.workhouses.org.uk
  Comprehensive introduction

- Rossbret Institutions Website
  www.institutions.org.uk
  Includes pages on Poor Law Unions, Workhouses, *etc.*

- Poor Law Union Database
  www.fourbears.worldonline.co.uk/Database.html
  Gazetteer

- Index to Paupers in Workhouses, 1861 (10% sample)
  www.genuki.org.uk/big/eng/Paupers/
  Sample of entries in a Parliamentary paper (see below, p.178)

Friendly Societies
- Friendly Societies Research Group
  www.open.ac.uk/socialsciences/fsrg/

Trade Unions
- Modern Records Centre
  ww2.warwick.ac.uk/services/library/mrc/

Further Reading
- COLE, ANNE. *Poor Law documents before 1834.* 2nd ed. F.F.H.S., 2000.
- GIBSON, JEREMY, *et al. Poor law union records.* 4 vols. F.F.H.S., 1997-2000.

- PALEY, RUTH. *My ancestor was a bastard.* Society of Genealogists, 2004.
- REID, ANDY. *The union workhouse: a study guide for teachers and local historians.* Learing local history **3**. Phillimore, for the British Association for Local History, 1994.
- SOKOLL, THOMAS. ed. *Essex pauper letters 1731-1837.* Records of social and economic history. New series **30**. Oxford University Press, 2001.
- LOGAN, ROGER. *An introduction to friendly society records.* F.F.H.S., 2000.
- SOUTHALL, HUMPHREY, GILBERT, DÀVID, & BRYCE, CAROL. *Nineteenth century trade union records: an introduction and select guide.* Historical geography research series **27**. Institute of British Geographers, Historical Georgraphy Research Group, 1994.

Chapter 12

Newspapers & Journals

Newspapers and journals contain an enormous amount of information of relevance to family historians. Birth, marriage and death notices are the most obvious features of relevance. Formal notices did, of course, have to be paid for, and hence those of humble means are unlikely to appear in such announcements. Obituaries, also usually concerned with the well-to-do, with people who were eminent or well-known, provide potted biographies of the deceased, and are likely to include dates of birth, family details, and discussion of the person's role in the social, political or religious groups with which he was associated. Accounts of funerals may be even more useful; they may include the names of all the mourners, sometimes with their relationship to the deceased, together with much other information. Such accounts are still to be read in the newspapers of some rural areas. When probate was granted, the value of the estate might be printed in both local and national newspapers. If a coroner's inquest was held, that too might be reported. Reports of weddings similarly often included details of the guests, and give details of the best man, parents, bridesmaids, pageboys, ushers, *etc.* Much more information used to be given than is usual today.

The information capable of being gleaned from newspapers is, however, much wider than just births, marriages and deaths. The proceedings of courts of law were regularly reported, and if your ancestor became entangled with the arm of the law, the fact is likely to be reported in the local newspaper. Reports of accidents, disasters, bankruptcies, crime, civic celebrations, council proceedings, *etc., etc.,* are all likely to include people's names. If your ancestors were tradesmen, they may well have inserted advertisements in the press, and these too should be checked out.

Newspapers may have a view on any subject you care to mention; they are opinionated; their factual content is not always to be relied upon. Their evidence must be carefully assessed for its veracity. Nevertheless, they do contain an enormous amount of information, and it is likely that most people have been mentioned in them at some time or other. The major problem for the family historian is to find the places where their ancestors are mentioned.

The first step is to identify the newspapers which covered the areas where your ancestors lived. This is best done by consulting the catalogue of the British Library's Newspaper Library at Colindale, which is available on the internet, and also in book format. This is the major national repository for newspapers; however, local studies libraries usually hold at least some runs of newspapers for their own area. A select union list of local newspapers prior to 1920 is provided by Gibson, *et al.;* Dixon is solely concerned with the nineteenth century. More comprehensive union lists are provided in the *Newsplan* reports, published by the British Library, which are part of a major project to preserve and microfilm newspapers. When you have identified the newspaper you wish to consult, you may find that you have to read it on microfilm.

Journals

It may also be helpful to consult journals, which were published less frequently than newspapers. The best known of these was probably the *Gentleman's Magazine,* issued monthly from 1730 to 1868, and described in detail by Christie; copies are widely available in major reference libraries. It included many notices of births, marriages and deaths, and also printed numerous obituaries, bankruptcy notices, announcements of new appointments in the army and the church, *etc.* Each annual volume is indexed; Nangle provides a consolidated index for the early years of the century.

Another important journal which deserves mention is the *London gazette.* This was published daily by the government throughout the nineteenth century, and contains official announcements such as appointments in government, the army and the church, medal awards, bankruptcy notices, lists of persons in various professions subject to government regulation, changes of name, *etc., etc.*

A wide variety of other journals contain useful information. For example, most religious denominations issued their own journals, which often included information on matters such as the movement of clergy and the names of church officers, *etc.* The growing interest in history led to the foundation of many county societies which published their own *transactions* giving lists of their officers, members, *etc.,* as well as many obituaries of antiquarians and even genealogists. The journals of trade unions and friendly societies included much similar information. If your ancestor was involved in a particular profession, it may well be worth checking the trade journals for an obituary, or for information on his movements.

Indexes

The major problem facing those who need to use newspapers in historical research is the sheer bulk of the material available. To know that a needle is certainly to be found is no comfort when searching a hay-stack! If indexes are not available, it is probably best to identify specific events, with dates, that you wish to check. And be warned that it is easy to be distracted from your search by information that has nothing to do with your family!

Indexes to newspapers have been few and far between. Fortunately, a number of indexing projects have been commenced in recent years. The indexes to the *Times* are a particularly valuable resource, including references to obituaries, birth, marriage and death notices, inquests, court cases, *etc., etc.* These are widely available in reference libraries as well as the subscription service on the internet. Indexes to other newspapers are listed in Gibson, *et al.* The British Library's Newspaper Library keeps a record of newspaper indexes; inquiries may also be made of local studies libraries and family history societies. A few extracts from newspapers have also been reprinted in recent years; a good example is Janice Simon's *Marriage & obituary notices 1848* (Kings Lynn: Janice Simons, 1992), which includes notices from the *Lynn Advertiser,* the *Wisbech Constitutional Gazette,* and the *Norfolk & Cambridgeshire Herald.* A very few extracts - again, mainly nineteenth-century - are available on the internet; it is likely that many more such web-pages will become available in the next few years. The British Library, for example, has a project to digitise up to 2,000,000 pages of nineteenth century newspapers.

Web Pages:
- British Library Newspapers
  www.bl.uk/collections/newspapers.html

- Newsplan
  www.bl.uk/collections/nplan.html

- Index to the Times
edina.ac.uk/times-index/
Subscription service only

Further Reading:
Introductory
- CHAPMAN, COLIN R. *Using newspapers and periodicals.* F.F.H.S., 1993.
- MURPHY, MICHAEL. *Newspapers and local history.* Phillimore, for the British Association for Local History, 1991.
- COLLINS, AUDREY. *Using Colindale and other newspaper repositories.* Basic facts about ... series F.F.H.S., 2001.

Lists
- GIBSON, JEREMY, LANGSTON, BRETT, & SMITH, BRENDA W. *Local newspapers 1750-1920, England and Wales, Channel Islands, Isle of Man: a select location list.* 2nd ed. F.F.H.S., 2002.
- DIXON, D. *Local newspapers & periodicals of the nineteenth century: a checklist of holdings in provincial libraries.* Victorian Studies handlist **6.** Leicester: University of Leicester Victorian Studies Centre, 1973.

Journals & Indexes
- CHRISTIE, P. 'The *Gentleman's Magazine* as a source for the family historian', *Genealogists magazine* **20,** 1981, 238-9.

- NANGLE, B. *The Gentleman's Magazine biographical and obituary notices, 1781-1819: an index.* New York: Garland, 1980.
- *Palmer's index to the Times newspaper, 1790-1922.* The Times, 1868-1925. Also available on CD.

Chapter 13

Trade Directories

The importance of lists of names is discussed in a number of other chapters of this book. The census, electoral registers, tax lists, *etc.,* all provide valuable information. Trade directories provide another type of name list, normally including addresses and occupations. They also include much useful background information. Details of carriers, railways, churches, local officials, *etc., etc.,* are usually included, but their principal objective was the promotion of commerce, and hence they list the substantial inhabitants who sustained that commerce.

The earliest directory was published in 1677, but it was not until the beginning of the nineteenth century that they began to come into their own. A number covering the whole country or large regions were published before 1800, but the earliest county directories were generally later; for example, the earliest for Lancashire was issued in 1818, for Kent 1803, for Devon as late as 1848. Far more directories were published in the last two decades of the century than had been the case in previous decades.

In the early nineteenth century, James Pigot was the leading directory publisher; his business was continued by his partner, Isaac Slater. In 1853, the business was taken over by the major rival firm run by Frederick Kelly, which continued its activities into the twentieth century. These publishers between them issued directories for most counties in England and Wales.

Pigot conducted five great surveys covering the whole of Britain between 1820 and 1853 although he ceased to compete with Kellys in London after 1840. His directories were generally regional; sometimes the same information was included in two or more different 'regional' volumes. This fact may not be immediately apparent to the researcher, since, in libraries, these directories have frequently been disbound so that the portions for each county can be stored and used separately; title pages have frequently been lost. This also applies to Kelly's directories; these were also issued as regional directories; however, the same information was frequently also issued in county volumes. Frederick Kelly took over the *Post Office London directory* in 1836 and began the publication of provincial directories with his *Directory of the six home counties* in 1845. The county series of Kelly's directories for most counties began in the 1850's and 1860's; new editions were issued every five to ten years until the mid-twentieth century. There were, for example, 18 editions of *Kelly's directory of Devonshire* between 1856 and 1939, and 22 editions of *Kelly's directory of Warwickshire* between 1854 and 1930.

These were not, of course, the only publishers. There were a number of smaller firms, such as William White, who issued 88 volumes between 1850 and 1919. There were also many local directory publishers; in Exeter, Besley's issued their first directory for the city in 1828, and continued to issue them regularly into the twentieth century.

The compilers of directories came from a wide range of backgrounds, and their aims were not necessarily identical. This is reflected in the diversity of approach to the task of compilation which they adopted, and the ways in which they decided on what information to include. Post Office officials saw the need for directories for postal purposes, and a variety of 'Post Office' directories were issued. These directories were the result of private initiative by Post Office staff; they were not officially sanctioned. Indeed, Frederick Kelly's use of Post Office staff to compile directories led to questions in the House of Commons.

Other publishers had cultural and historical interests; short historical notes were a feature of many directories, but a number of directories were issued in conjunction with major historical works. In 1822 Edward Baines and William Parson issued their *History, directory and gazetteer of Yorkshire,* a combination which they, their successor, William White, and a number of imitators continued to make for many years.

Another approach was that adopted by Isaac Cottrill, a policeman in Newcastle under Lyme. The directory he published in 1836 was originally compiled for his own use as a policeman.

Despite these different approaches, the major distinguishing characteristic of trade directories is that they were compiled for commercial purposes. They were intended to promote trade. They provided tradesmen and shop-keepers with the names of potential customers; they enabled potential customers to identify the businesses who could supply their needs. There were, of course, other uses: magistrates, clergy, and local officials might consult them for administrative purposes; visitors and antiquarians might use them to identify places worth visiting; they might be used for geographical purposes, or simply to locate a particular individual. Their primary purpose, however, was to enable tradesmen and their customers to contact each other, and this fact governed who was included or excluded.

The content and format of directories generally follow a common pattern. County directories generally have a separate entry for each village or parish, which includes a brief historical and topographical account, with notes on topics such as the church, the post office, carriers, schools, *etc.,* and the names of local office holders such as the rector, J.P.'s, poor law officers, registrars, *etc.* This will be followed by an alphabetical listing of the principal inhabitants, that is, the farmers and landowners, the leading tradesmen, and those of 'independent means'. The list will only include heads of households; it will not include servants, labourers or other employees, nor will it list women, unless they are widows with property.

Town directories are somewhat more inclusive; they generally include street lists, together with separate lists of particular trades, and / or alphabetical lists of all tradesmen. Again, the list consists of heads of households only. All householders on the principal streets are likely to be listed, but alleyways and side roads might be missed.

Directories record the social structure of the upper and middle classes, i.e. the people who were likely to need the goods which tradesmen could provide. Those at the bottom of the social hierarchy were excluded. If you can find no mention of your ancestor in a directory, it does not mean that he was not present in the community; he may simply have been a servant or employee.

The process of compiling and publishing directories may cause problems to the modern researcher. The information provided was frequently obtained by canvassing, although it may also have been obtained from knowledgeable local people, such as the postmen mentioned above. Whatever method was used, there was far more room for error than was the case with the census (which was itself not free of error). Furthermore, the process of collecting the information took time; directories could easily be six months out of date on publication. Those reprinted from previous editions would obviously be much more out of date than that, so it may pay to check the status of each directory you use. When was it published? When was it compiled? Is it a reprint? With luck, you may find this information in the directory itself, or perhaps in the bibliographies listed at the end of this chapter.

Trade directories may yield a great deal of information for your family history. The information in them should always be compared with that in the census, and in other sources. If there is a run of directories they may enable you to trace where your ancestors lived for much of the century, or to keep track of them between censuses. They may also be used to identify the homes of family names across wide areas, and thus to discover other places where it might be worthwhile to undertake further research.

Norton lists 878 directories for the period to 1855; Tipper and Shaw list a further 2,200 for the period to 1950, although the majority of these relate to the twentieth century. Both books indicate locations. The county volumes of Raymond's *British genealogical library guides* also give comprehensive lists of published directories. Substantial collections are held by the British Library, the Guildhall Library, and the Society of Genealogists. Most local studies libraries have many directories for their own areas, as have some record offices. It is, however, rare to find provincial libraries holding many directories from other areas - although there is a good nation-wide collection at Birmingham Public Library. Most directories are rare; only a few copies have survived. Indeed, it is likely that many early directories have been lost entirely. And it is unlikely that you will be able to borrow directories via inter-library loan, with the exception of the handful that have had paper reprints. However, innumerable directories are now available on microform or CD's; full lists are given in Raymond's listings of these formats (see chapter 1 further reading). Most publishers of fiche and CD's have their own websites, and these should be checked for the latest information.

Many directories are also available on the internet. The most important site in this regard is undoubtedly the University of Leicester's *Digital Library of Historical Directories*. The university's library has a substantial collection of directories, hundreds of which are now available in digitised form. The web site also includes a powerful search engine, capable of finding the names of individuals and families.

Many extracts from directories are given on Genuki local pages (**www.genuki.org.uk**). The web pages of local studies libraries sometimes list their holdings of directories. A number of other sites for trade directories are listed in Raymond's *Family history on the web.*

Web Sites
- Digital Library of Historical Directories
  www.historicaldirectories.org

Further Reading

- NORTON, JANE E. *Guide to the national and provincial directories of England and Wales, excluding London, published before 1856.* Royal Historical Society guides and handbooks **5**. 1950.
- SHAW, GARETH, & TIPPER, ALLISON. *British directories: a bibliography and guide to directories published in England and Wales (1850-1950) and Scotland (1773-1950.* Leicester University Press, 1988.
- NEWINGTON-IRVINE, N.J.N. *Directories and poll-books, including almanacs and electoral rolls, in the library of the Society of Genealogists.* Library sources **5**. 6th ed. Society of Genealogists, 1995.
- ATKINS, P.J. *The directories of London, 1677-1977.* Mansell, 1990.
- WEBB, CLIFF. *Surrey directories: a finding list.* Research aids **29**. West Surrey Family History Society, 1994.
- MILLS, DENNIS R. *Rural community history from trade directories.* Aldenham: Local Population Studies, 2001.

Chapter 14

Official Lists of Names

List of names, especially when they include addresses, are vital sources of information for family historians. They enable the researcher to locate particular surnames in time and place, and thus provide vital clues for further research. If a list states that the Weaver family was to be found in Buckland Dinham in 1832, then the probability is that a search of other records for that parish - parish registers, the 1841 census, monumental inscriptions, *etc.* - might also yield information.

Many of the sources already discussed are, in effect, lists of names. The focus of this chapter will be on those lists produced for official purposes, and especially on poll books, electoral registers and tax lists.

Poll Books & Electoral Registers

At the end of the eighteenth century, the law required sheriffs, as returning officers, to compile lists of voters - poll books - in Parliamentary elections, indicating the candidates for whom they had cast their votes. Voting was regarded as a public duty, and hence the way in which voters cast their votes was open to public scrutiny: the idea that ballots should be secret was not accepted until 1872.

England had been divided into Parliamentary constituencies in the medieval period. Each county was a constituency in its own right, returning two M.P.'s (one in the Welsh constituencies). Most Parliamentary boroughs, mainly in the South, also returned two members. This structure remained in place until the Reform Act 1832, which divided most counties into two or more constituencies, and gave much greater representation to the industrial towns of the north. The Reform Act also required the compilation of electoral registers, specifying the names of those entitled to vote. Between 1832 and 1868, both electoral registers and poll books may be available; 1868 saw the last general election before the introduction of the secret ballot, and the consequent cessation of poll books.

The right to vote depended on a property qualification for most of the century, although this was modified in several acts. Prior to 1832, the county electorate was confined to those who owned land worth forty shillings per annum. In the boroughs, the qualification varied; in a very few places (Westminster being an important example) it extended to most heads of household, but in other places it might be confined to the freemen, or to members of the borough council. It was a matter of local custom, or perhaps of the borough charter. The 1832 act extended the franchise to leaseholders and copy holders, *etc.,* and made it uniform. Further extensions of the franchise took place in 1867, when householders in boroughs were enfranchised, and in 1884, when rural householders were also included. But universal suffrage had to wait until the twentieth century.

Poll books record the names and votes of those who cast their votes in Parliamentary elections. Not all were printed; some survive in manuscript. There was no uniform method of presentation; the information they contain, and the order in which it is presented, vary. County poll books are likely to be arranged by hundred/wapentake, and then by parish; borough poll books perhaps by ward, or simply alphabetically. Where alphabetical order is adopted it may only apply to initial letters, entries being apparently random after the first letter. Usually places of residence are given, but not necessarily addresses as such: i.e. the parish only may be given. However, the place of the freehold which gave the right to vote is often stated; if it was tenanted, the name of the tenant is occasionally given. Occupations are also frequently stated.

A full listing of surviving poll books is given by Gibson & Rogers. Major collections are held by the British Library, the Institute of Historical Research, Guildhall Library and the Society of Genealogists. Most county record offices and/or local studies libraries hold poll books for their own localities. A number have been reprinted by the present author, and also by a few family history societies and CD publishers.

Electoral registers began in 1832, and were issued

annually for the rest of the century. They list those entitled to vote, rather than votes actually cast. Voters were numbered and listed alphabetically by polling district. Their names were given in full, together with places of abode, the nature of the qualification to vote, and the identity of the property which gave that qualification, or perhaps the name of its tenant. Sometimes there are separate lists for property owners and occupiers; there may also be separate lists for those with a lodger's franchise after 1885; these include the names of landlords and landladies, the weekly rent, and the number of rooms rented. All lists should be checked. Changes in the dates on which registers came into force may prove confusing; in both 1868 and 1885 two successive registers came into force, the first on 1st January in each year, the second on 1st November and 7th November respectively.

There may also be separate registers for local elections, i.e. for borough councils, county councils (from 1884) and parish councils (from 1894), and perhaps also for poor law guardians, school boards, *etc.* The franchise for these elections varied from that for Parliamentary elections, and hence separate registers were sometimes needed. Alternatively, registers may be marked to indicate voters who were not entitled to vote in particular elections.

The fact that electoral registers are annual means that they can be used to trace movements between each decennial census. Their dating, however, needs to be understood. They list those who were qualified to vote on 31st July (or 15th July between 1878 and 1884) of the year <u>before</u> the register came into force. That is therefore the date which genealogists will need to use, rather than the dates during which the register was in force (which are listed by Gibson & Rogers and by Cheffins). There could easily be changes by removal or death between these dates.

After 1878, burgess rolls could be merged with electoral registers: since these were in street order the alphabetical arrangement of registers often lapsed. Compilation was undertaken by the parochial overseers of the poor, who based their work on the rate books and personal knowledge.

Electoral registers survive in quantity in local studies libraries and county record offices, although they often have gaps in coverage. Small collections are also by the Society of Genealogists, the Guildhall Library, and the National Archives; these are all listed by Gibson and Rogers. Their book does not, however, list the extensive collection held by the British Library; for that, reference must be made to Cheffins.

Tax Lists
Nobody likes paying taxes. However, the pain suffered by taxpayers in previous centuries has frequently resulted in valuable information for the family historian. For the nineteenth century, there were a number of imposts for which some records survive;

these included the land tax, the income tax, and local rates.

The land tax was first levied in 1692, and continued to be levied until 1963. Assessments were made every year, and list the names of landowners and occupiers parish by parish. These names should be treated with caution for two reasons. Firstly, they are not always up to date, and it is wise to cross-check them with the burial register. The word 'late' before a name may indicate a death or a sale of land. Secondly, long-term leaseholders and copyholders may be described as 'proprietors or owners' rather than as occupiers. Assessments show the amount assessed and perhaps the rateable value (which was assessed in the late seventeenth century and remained unchanged until the tax was abolished); they may also provide a description of the property, or note that the tax was due on tithes, excise officer salaries, *etc.* Taxpayers may appear in the assessments more than once; if they owned more than one property, an assessment would be made on each property. Finally, the assessments record (until 1832) property which had been exonerated from the tax. An act of 1798 permitted commutation of the land tax in return for a lump sum payment of fifteen years tax. Tax which had been commuted is recorded in redemption certificates (IR 24) and parish books of redemption (IR 22), held by the National Archives. They also hold copies of all the assessments for 1798-9 (IR 23), which resulted from the 1798 act.

Until the 1832 Reform Act, duplicates of the land tax were used by the Clerk of the Peace, who was responsible for listing voters. Consequently, these duplicates survive in quantity amongst Quarter Sessions records. After 1832, survival of assessments is much more spasmodic; furthermore, they cease to record all land-holdings, since there was no longer a need to include a record of land tax commuted. Gibson & Mills provide a listing of surviving assessments.

The importance of the land tax as a genealogical source decreases as the nineteenth century progresses. Its place may be taken by the records of local rating. Rates were imposed for a variety of local tasks: relief of the poor, maintainance of the church, sewers (i.e. drainage), *etc.* They were collected by parish officers, or, in towns, by borough officials, and in the nineteenth century are often recorded in purposely printed rate books, which may be found with the parish and borough records in county record offices.

Rate books give information that is similar in character to that found in land tax assessments. They list householders and/or owners, with an assessment of the value of their property, and the amount due to be collected from them. Usually, these lists are arranged street by street, and in the order of the houses in the street. Each years' rate book tends to be based on the one before it. If a series of rate books is available, it may be possible to identify the specific house in which an ancestor lived, and the dates he was there.

A variety of other taxes were imposed in the nineteenth century, but most left limited records. Income tax, is a typical example. Returns for 1799-1816, giving names of taxpayers by parish, are held in the National Archives (E 182). Otherwise, most returns have been destroyed. However, Colley discovered and printed assessments found in a county record office, and it is quite possible that similar collections of assessments await discovery.

Web Pages
• United Kingdom Electoral Registers and their Uses
  www.bl.uk/collections/social/spis_er.html

Further Reading
Poll Books
• GIBSON, JEREMY, & ROGERS, COLIN. *Poll books c.1696-1872: a directory to holdings in Great Britain.* 2nd ed. F.F.H.S., 1990.
• SIMS, JOHN, ed. *A handlist of British Parliamentary poll books.* Occasional publications **4.** University of Leicester History Dept., 1984.

Electoral Registers
• GIBSON, JEREMY, & ROGERS, COLIN. *Electoral registers since 1832, and burgess rolls.* 2nd ed. F.F.H.S., 1990.
• CHEFFINS, R.H.A. *Parliamentary constituencies and their registers since 1832.* British Library, 1998.

Land Tax

- GIBSON, JEREMY, & MILLS, DENNIS. *Land tax assessments c.1690-c.1950.* F.F.H.S., 1983.
- UNWIN, R.W. *Search guide to the English land tax.* West Yorkshire County Record Office, 1982.
- GINTER, DONALD E. *A measure of wealth: the English land tax in historical analysis.* Hambledon Press, 1992.

Rates

- DARLINGTON, IDA. 'Rate books,' in MUNBY, L.M., ed. *Short guide to records, first series, guides 1-24.* [Rev.ed]. Historical Association, 1994, 21-4.

Income Tax

- COLLEY, ROBERT, ed. *Devizes Division income tax assessments, 1842-1860.* Wiltshire Record Society **54**. 2002.

Chapter 15

Educational Records

Education in nineteenth century England underwent drastic changes. At the beginning of the century, there was no state involvement in education. By its end, every child was required to attend school until the age of thirteen. The Sunday School movement grew from c.750,000 pupils in 1795 to over 6,000,000 in 1900. Voluntary societies established at the beginning of the century established a wide network of elementary schools, many of which received state aid from 1833. The nonconformist British & Foreign Schools Society (1800) and its Anglican rival, the National Society for the Education of the Poor (1811) were the most important of these; they also undertook teacher training. Schools were also established by some poor law unions for the education of pauper children in their care. In 1870 the government established local school boards to fill the gaps in elementary education left by these societies and unions.

The records created as a result of this activity are extensive, but information of use to family historians is uncommon for the first half of the century. The names of pupils who attended Sunday schools and the early voluntary-elementary schools rarely survive, although from the mid-century onwards there are sometimes admission books and attendance registers to be found in Methodist circuit and chapel archives (held by county record offices). Similar records may be found amongst the records of other denominations. Admission registers, discharge orders and school attendance papers for poor law schools may sometimes be found with union records. Teachers are better provided for; the careers of those trained by the British & Foreign Schools Society can usually be traced through its records.

Record keeping improved from 1862, when the government required schools in receipt of government grants to maintain log books. These were intended to be records of day to day activities, and included many notes on the progress (or otherwise) of individual pupils. An example from Whitchurch has been edited by Horn. Subsequently, the post-1870 board schools were required to maintain admission registers, which recorded the names of children and their parents (although not always the mother), their address, the child's date of birth, details of any previous school, and the dates of admission and leaving, perhaps with a note on where the child was to begin work. The great majority of late nineteenth century children are likely to be mentioned in these registers, which have usually been deposited in county record offices.

There are also many records relating to schools which received government support in the National

Archives. It is rare for these records to actually name pupils, although they can reveal much background information. Details are given by Morton.

Secondary education in nineteenth-century England was generally for the middle and upper classes, who paid for it. The great public schools, such as Eton and Harrow, attracted the sons of the governing classes; yeomen and the lesser gentry sent their children to local grammar schools. Many of these schools have published registers of their pupils; indeed, in some instances there are several editions (all of which should be checked). Many histories have also been published; these usually give lists of masters, and sometimes include details of pupils as well. Jacobs provides a detailed list of registers, and the catalogue of the extensive collection held by the Society of Genealogists has also been published. Wallis and Cunningham between them list published school histories. Raymond's county bibliographies also include listings of published works.

Students who continued their education at university are easily traced. The biographical dictionaries of Foster and Venn for Oxford and Cambridge respectively list all students at those universities, usually indicating birthplaces and parentage, and including brief notes on their subsequent carrers. Registers of the other universities founded during the century are also available; details are provided by Jacobs.

Further Reading
General
- CHAPMAN, COLIN R. *The growth of British education and its records.* 2nd ed. Lochin Publishing, 1992.
- STEPHENS, W.B., & UNWIN, R.W. *Materials for the local and regional study of schooling.* Archives and the user **7.** British Records Association, 1987.
- MORTON, ANN. *Education and the state from 1833.* P.R.O. Readers guide **18.** P.R.O. Publications, 1997.
- HORN, PAMELA. 'School log books', in THOMPSON, K.M., ed. *Short guides to records: second series, guides 25-48.* Historical Association, 1997, 104-8.
- HORN, PAMELA, ed. *Village education in nineteenth-century Oxfordshire: the Whitchurch school log book (1868-93) and other documents.* Oxfordshire Record Society **51.** 1979.

Bibliographies
- JACOBS, P.M. *Registers of the universities, colleges and schools of Great Britain and Ireland: a list.* Athlone Press, 1966.
- *School, university and college registers in the library of the Society of Genealogists.* 2nd ed. Society of Genealogists, 1988.
- CUNNINGHAM, PETER. *Local history of education in England and Wales: a bibliography.* University of Leeds Museum of the History of Education, 1976.
- WALLIS, J. *Histories of old schools: a revised list for England and Wales.* University of Newcastle Dept. of Education, 1966.

University Registers

- VENN, J.A. *Alumni Cantabrigienses: a biographical list of all known students, graduates, and holders of office at the University of Cambridge, from the earliest times to 1900. Part II, from 1752 to 1900.* 6 vols. Cambridge University Press, 1940-54.
- FOSTER, JOSEPH. *Alumni Oxonienses, 1500-1886.* 8 vols. Parker & Co., 1887-92. Reprinted in 4 vols, Kraus Reprint, 1980.
- FOSTER, JOSEPH. *Oxford men 1880-1892, with a record of their schools honours and degrees.* Oxford: John Parker & Sons, 1893.

Chapter 16

Records of Landowners & Occupiers

Most of our ancestors lived in houses, and occupied specific pieces of land. The records of landownership and occupation can therefore be made to yield valuable information about them. Many of the records already discussed - census records, civil registration certificates, *etc.* - provide incidental information about places of residence; the land tax returns sometimes provide more detailed information on ownership over a period, if they have survived. Similar information is given by enclosure awards and tithe apportionments, which will be considered here, as will fire insurance policy records. Perhaps the most useful information in this context, however, is provided by estate records - deeds, leases, rentals, surveys, *etc.* These survive in great quantity in both county record offices and the National Archives, and also in institutions such as the British Library, university libraries, and a variety of specialist repositories. They may also be found in some overseas repositories.

Estate Records
Locating estate records is, to a certain extent, a matter of serendipity. The relevant county record office should always be checked, together with any other

important local collections, such as may be held in university and public libraries. The *Index of manuscripts in the British Library* (10 vols. Chadwyck-Healey, 1984) is also worth checking. The National Archives holds innumerable deeds, *etc.,* as do a wide variety of other repositories, including a number of institutions in North America and Australia.

Alcock devotes an entire chapter to the question of locating deeds. There are also, a number of web pages which offer substantial assistance. It should be easy to trace manorial records through the Manorial Documents Register. Two invaluable databases, A2A and Archives Hub (see pp. 17-18), index a rapidly increasing number of archival calendars issued by county record offices, and by the manuscript departments of university and college libraries respectively. The database of the National Register of Archives is also worth consulting. The web pages of particular institutions are also worth checking; they frequently provide detailed listings of holdings.

A wide variety of documents may be found in estate archives. The most common are title deeds, which often contain invaluable evidence concerning family relationships. The purpose of the deed was to provide secure title to property; this meant that the title of the seller had to be clearly demonstrated. If the property had been inherited, then the relationship of the seller to the previous purchaser had to be set out. If the property had been bequeathed by will then the will provided additional proof of title. There should also be an abstract of title, listing previous deeds, and summarising the ownership of the property over perhaps the previous couple of centuries.

There were a variety of types of deed, often written in legal jargon which may be difficult to follow for the uninitiated. The lease is probably the simplest to understand; it formalized the relationship between landowner and tenant. It was retained by the landowner; the tenant received a copy known as the counterpart lease. It set out the term of the lease, the amounts to be paid for entry fine and rent, and any other conditions in the tenancy.

The lease and release must not be confused with the ordinary lease. The former was perhaps the most common, indeed, almost the only, type of conveyance in the early nineteenth century, but its use was abolished by the Real Property Act, 1845. Two documents were involved, the lease for a year, and the release. The latter was a sale of the reversion of the property to the leaseholder, executed on the day after the lease, and making the leaseholder the only person with an interest in the property.

Some land continued to be held by copyhold tenure throughout the nineteenth century. The copyhold tenant held by virtue of a copy of the manorial court roll. By this date, this was virtually equivalent to freehold tenure, but changes in ownership had to be recorded on the court roll, which can easily be located by consulting the Manorial Documents register (see its web page).

The final concord also survived into the nineteenth century, but was finally abolished in 1833. Fines are records of fictitious actions at law in the Court of Common Pleas, undertaken in order that a conveyance might be registered in the court. Three indented copies were made, for the buyer, the seller, and the court (copies in the court are known as feet of fines). Much of the information in fines is totally fictitious, or highly inaccurate; however, they may provide useful genealogical information. A fine may be accompanied by a deed to lead the uses of a fine, which explain its purpose.

Private deeds could also be registered on the Chancery Close Rolls, now in the National Archives (C54). Such registration continued throughout the nineteenth century, although it dwindled after the establishment of the Land Registry in 1862. Registration of title in the Land Registry was voluntary until 1899, but it did offer secure title. Secure title was also offered by the deeds registries which operated throughout the century in the three Yorkshire ridings, in the Bedford Levels, and in Middlesex. No genealogist tracing ancestors in these areas should neglect these registries.

A variety of other forms of conveyancing can be found amongst nineteenth-century records. Alcock provides a detailed guide; briefer summaries are offered by Dibben and Cornwall.

Estate records may also include surveys, rentals, accounts, and various other documents. These too may yield useful information for the family historian, providing interesting details of farms and property. Surveys, which may have maps attached, are detailed descriptions of property field by field; they name tenants, and may name their predecessors (which is helpful if they are relatives). Information on leases in force at the time of the survey may also be given.

Rentals are briefer than surveys; generally they name tenants, acreages and rents. They were often compiled at regular intervals; if a run of rentals can be found, the succession of tenants can be worked out from them, and several generations of the same family may be found.

Estate and household accounts may also record rents received; they are also likely to be useful for a much broader range of information, and may be full of names. It may be possible to use them to trace agricultural labourers and servants between censuses. They may record the payment of masons for building work, doctors for medical care, tradesmen for goods supplied, *etc., etc.*. Household accounts often provide the raw material to reconstruct the daily life of the family they belonged to.

Enclosure
The late eighteenth and early nineteenth centuries were the great age of the Parliamentary enclosure movement, which altered the face of the English

landscape. Open fields, which had been farmed in common, were replaced by enclosures farmed in severalty. In the nineteenth century, this was usually effected by act of Parliament, which normally provided for the appointment of a commission to assess the rights of landowners, survey the land, and divide it into individual plots so that each person with an interest received a holding of appropriate size and value. The major documents which resulted from this process were maps and awards. These may usually be found in county record offices; some were also enrolled at Westminster, and are in the National Archives (C 54 or E 13). From 1845, a permanent Enclosure Commission was established; it retained copies of all maps and awards, which are now in MAF 1. Tate provides a full listing of surviving records.

For the family historian, enclosure awards provide useful listings of local landowners and tenants; in conjunction with the maps, they provide detailed descriptions of individual farms. Typically, awards begin with written copies of the signed oaths taken by the commissioners, and perhaps by the surveyor. A preamble will describe how the commissioners have carried out their work. Parish boundaries may then be described, followed by details of arrangements for roads and drainage *etc.,* laid down by the commissioners. The main sections of awards deal with the allocation of land in the new enclosures to the proprietors. These are generally listed in order of status: the lord of the manor first, followed by the incumbent and any other major landowner, then the tenants of substantial farms, followed by cottagers who might have perhaps a quarter of an acre. Some of those listed may have received two allotments, one in their own right, one in the right of their wives, who could not own land in their own names. Land might also be vested in the churchwardens and the overseers to support the church and the poor. Awards conclude with general instructions to the proprietors on their rights and obligations, and signatures of the commissioners.

Tithe Apportionments

Tithe apportionments, from the family historians point of view, provide similar information to that found in enclosure awards. However, they had a totally different origin. Tithes were theoretically a payment of one-tenth of the land's produce paid for the support of the church, or, more strictly, of parochial incumbents. By the nineteenth century, the system was riddled with anomalies, and the Tithe Commutation Act 1836 provided for the commutation of tithes to a rent-charge. That involved the calculation of rent charges and its division between landowners, and necessitated the survey of most parishes, the drawing of a map, and the making of an apportionment listing the names of those liable to pay, with the amounts due. Sandell has edited the apportionments for Wiltshire, and his book provides a useful example of the information available.

Tithe maps and apportionments are now in the National Archives (IR 29 and IR 30), and have been listed by the List and Index Society; they usually have to be consulted on microfilm or fiche. Copies were also prepared for the parish and the bishop; these are generally in county record offices. Apportionments were written on printed forms, with columns for 'occupiers', 'numbers referring to the plan', 'name and description of land and premises', 'quantities in statute measure', 'amount of rent-charge apportioned upon the several lands, and payable to ...', and 'remarks'. The 'numbers' refer to the tithe map; every field is listed, and can be identified on the map.

Most apportionments and maps were compiled between 1838 and 1854. It is therefore possible to use them to make comparisons with the 1841 and 1851 censuses. Unfortunately, it may not be possible to compare them with earlier enclosure awards, since the latter frequently extinguished tithes.

Fire Insurance

Information relating to the proprietors of land can also be found in the ledgers of insurance companies. Fire insurance began in the eighteenth century, and was a major business in our period. The policy registers of insurance companies may provide a great deal of information on the properties and businesses of policy holders. Many of these registers have been deposited in record offices; the Guildhall Library has a particularly strong collection. Cockerell and Green provide a detailed list of records; as does Hawkings. Many fire insurance records are also listed on the A2A web site.

A fire insurance policy is a contract to insure property or goods of a specified value against loss by fire. Policies therefore, give the names and addresses of policyholders, together with a detailed description of the property and / or goods insured, with values. They are likely to name the occupants of houses insured. If an original policy can be compared with successive renewals, the changing fortunes of the policy holder can be traced. Hawkings includes hundreds of examples from policy registers, and also describes in detail the various other records of insurance companies that may be of use.

Web Pages

- Manorial Documents Register
  www.mdr.nationalarchives.gov.uk/

- Land Conveyances: Enrolment of Deeds, and Registration of Title
  **www.catalogue.nationalarchives.gov.uk/
  RdLeaflet.asp?sLeafletID=148**

- The Middlesex Deeds Registry 1709-1938
  **www.cityoflondon.gov.uk/Corporation/
  leisure__heritage/libraries__archives__
  museums__galleries/lma/visitor__information/
  free__information__leaflets.htm**
  Click on title

- The East Riding Register of Deeds: a guide for users
  www.eastriding.gov.uk/libraries/archives/
                               pdf/deedsnet.pdf

- The West Riding Registry of Deeds
  www.archives.wyjs.org.uk/wrrdl.htm

- Enclosure Awards
  www.catalogue.nationalarchives.gov.uk/
                  RdLeaflet.asp?sLeafletID=252

- Tithe Records
  www.catalogue.nationalarchives.gov.uk/
                  RdLeaflet.asp?sLeafletID=100

- Fire Insurance Records at Guildhall Library
  www.history.ac.uk/gh/fire.htm

Further Reading
Estate Records

- ALCOCK, N.W. *Old title deeds: a guide for local and family history.* 2nd ed. Phillimore, 2001.
- DIBBEN, A.A. *Title deeds, 13th-19th centuries.* Helps for students of history **72.** Historical Association, 1968.
- CORNWALL, J.C.K. *Reading old title deeds.* 2nd ed. F.F.H.S., 1997.
- SHEPPARD, F., & BELCHER, V. The deeds registries of Yorkshire and Middlesex', *Journal of the Society of Archivists* **6**(5), 1980, 274-86.

Enclosure Awards

- HOLLOWELL, STEVE. *Enclosure records for historians.* Phillimore, 2000.
- TATE, W.E. *A domesday of English enclosure acts and awards,* ed. M.E.Turner. Reading: University of Reading Library, 1978.
- TATE, W.E. 'Enclosure awards and acts', in MUNBY, L.M., ed. *Short guides to records. First series, guides 1-24.* [Rev. ed.] Historical Association, 1994, 77-8.

Tithe Apportionments & Maps

- EVANS, ERIC J., & CROSBY, ALAN G. *Tithes: maps, apportionments and the 1836 act: a guide for local historians.* 3rd ed. British Association for Local History, 1997.
- BEECH, GERALD, N.E. & MITCHELL, ROSE. *Maps for family and local history: a guide to the records of the tithe, Valuation Office and national farm surveys of England and Wales.* Readers guide **26.** National Archives, 2004.
- KAIN, ROGER J.T., & PRINCE, H.C. *Tithe surveys for historians.* Phillimore, 2000.
- *Inland Revenue: tithe maps and apportionments (IR29, IR30).* 2 vols. List and Index Society **68** & **83.** 1971-2.
- SANDELL, R.E., ed. *Abstracts of Wiltshire tithe apportionments.* Wiltshire Record Society **30.** 1975.

Fire Insurance Records

- COCKERELL, H.A.L., & GREEN, EDWIN. *The British insurance business: a guide to its history and records.* Sheffield Academic Press, 1994.
- THOMAS, J.H. 'Fire insurance policy registers', in MUNBY, L.M., ed. *Short guides to records: first series, guides 1-24.* Historical Association, 1994, 97-100.
- HAWKINGS, DAVID T. *Fire insurance records for family and local historians, 1696-1920.* Francis Boutle, 2003.

Chapter 17

Court Records

The records of courts of law contain a great deal of information of interest to family historians, although they are not always the easiest records to search. Hawkings has provided a detailed and valuable guide to tracing criminal ancestors; however, the records also provide much information on the other people caught up in the judicial process: judges, lawyers, police, witnesses, victims, *etc.* The records of civil cases may also throw much light on family history. It should also be borne in mind that the functions of some courts were much wider than those by courts today. In particular, Quarter Sessions were much more than merely courts of law; they played the prime role in county government.

Quarter Sessions

Before the establishment of county councils in 1889, the principle that executive and judicial powers should be exercised by separate bodies was not recognised in English county government. Quarter sessions directed the government of the county. They also sat as a court of law, dealing with both criminal and civil matters. The prime functions of the court were:

- the hearing of criminal trials where cases required a jury but were not of sufficient seriousness to require a trial before Assizes; also the hearing of civil cases, especially those concerning the poor law.
- the administration of county government. Prisons, asylums and bridges had to be maintained, a police force had to be managed, licences for various purposes had to be granted.
- to act as a public registry for various documents. Enclosure awards had to be registered, land tax records kept, deeds enrolled, poll books compiled.

In the course of the nineteenth century, there were many legislative changes affecting quarter sessions, notably the New Poor Law of 1834, which established poor law unions (see chapter 11), and the Local Government Act 1888, establishing county councils, which took over the non-judicial activities of the justices. Their judicial activities, however, increased, and many minor cases were diverted to petty sessions. These responsibilities generated an enormous quantity of records, which form the basis of the collections of county record offices. Some of these records have been discussed in other chapters. There are many others. Quarter sessions records can be divided into five broad categories:

- Order books: the formal record of court proceedings
- Sessions rolls and files: the documents actually used in court and also those which resulted from court orders. These include the rough minutes of

proceedings, i.e. sessions books, process books listing the names of those indicted, the accusations against them, and the court's verdict; they also include lists of those present, (including J.P.'s, jurors, prisoners, *etc.,*) writs, presentments, indictments, depositions, and petitions. Removal orders, sacrament certificates (recording oaths taken by clergy, churchwardens, *etc.,* before 1828) licence registers, *etc.,* resulted from the orders and activities of the court.

- Treasurers' accounts of receipts and payments, together with accounts of special funds such as those for bridges, roads, gaols, police, *etc.,* also bills and vouchers relating to expenses for, e.g. transport of felons, payment of officers, compensation paid to owners of slaughtered cattle (following the cattle plague of 1865 and subsequently).
- Other administrative records, such as registers of licences for gamekeepers, victuallers, pedlars and printing presses, registers of insolvent debtors, records concerning freemasons' lodges, minutes of committees for, e.g. highways, diseases of animals, lunatic asylums, *etc.,* gaol calendars, lists of pauper lunatics (etc.)
- Deposited records, including enrolled deeds, charity reports, land tax records, poll books, electoral registers, enclosure awards, *etc.*

These records are not easy for family historians to use, but do contain a mass of valuable information.

Unfortunately, most studies of them tend to relate to the centuries prior to 1800, although more survives for the nineteenth century. Gibson provides a detailed (but far from comprehensive) listing of records for each county. Emmison & Gray provides a useful introduction, as does McLaughlin, although both are primarily concerned with earlier centuries.

Assizes

The assize courts exercised criminal jurisdiction over the more serious offences throughout the nineteenth century. Cases were referred to them either from Quarter Sessions, or from the central courts in London. The assize judges travelled a circuit of several counties, in each of which they sat twice a year. Crown minute books, indictments, depositions, and some other records are held in the ASSI classes in the National Archives; details are given on the web page. The best place to start an inquiry is with the crown minute books, which provide summaries of each case, often noting the plea, verdict and sentence. Indictments provide similar information, but are more difficult to use. Depositions may contain much useful personal information.

Middlesex stood aside from the Assize circuits. It, together with the City of London, was under the jurisdiction of the Old Bailey, with the Lord Mayor acting as chief justice. Its records are principally in the Corporation of London Record Office (for the City of London) and the London Metropolitan Archives (for

Middlesex), although some are also in the National Archives (see the Old Bailey web page).

In 1834, the functions of the Old Bailey were taken over by the Central Criminal Court, whose jurisdiction was also extended to parts of Essex, Kent and Surrey. Its records are similar to those of the assize courts, and are held in the National Archives.

King's Bench (Criminal Jurisdiction)

The Court of King's Bench was the final court of appeal, until 1875. It had jurisdiction over all criminal cases, and supervisory powers over assizes and lesser courts; it also exercised a local jurisdiction in Middlesex. Its records are in the National Archives. They are difficult to use for family historians; however, there are separate indexes to London and Middlesex defendants, 1673-1843 (IND 1/6669-6677), and to provincial defendants, 1765-1843 (IND 1/6680-6684); there is also a card index to entries on the plea rolls (KB 28), 1844-59.

Civil Courts

Civil litigation also generated a mass of documentation which may be useful to the family historian. The records of the Court of Chancery, the King's Bench, the Court of Exchequer (to 1841) and the Supreme Court of Judicature (from 1875), are all in the National Archives; however, they are often difficult to use. Records tend to fall into three categories: the pleadings of litigants (bills, answers and replications), depositions, affidavits, *etc.,* of witnesses, and the decisions and reports of the courts. The depositions of witnesses are often the most useful source of information for researchers, and may give valuable information on family relationships and changes in fortune. The various web pages of the National Archives listed below give details of the numerous classes of documents concerned, and the indexes and other finding aids available. Horwitz also provides useful information on the records of the Court of Exchequer.

Coroners Records

Coroners have been required to investigate the circumstances of unnatural, sudden, or suspicious deaths since medieval times. Until 1888, most coroners were elected by freeholders; since then they have been appointed by local authorities. Until 1926 most inquests were held before a jury. The principal records of interest to genealogists are the reports of actual inquests. These give details of the deceased, the death, the names of the jury, and the verdict. There may also be witness statements. Registers of inquests note the inquest date, the deceased's name, address, and place of death. Most records are held in county record offices, and are listed by Gibson & Rogers. The National Archives does hold inquest records where a trial for murder or manslaughter was involved. Much documentation has been lost; however, reports of inquests may often be found in local newspapers (see chapter 12). If a date is known, this should be checked. Barnard prints many such reports.

Web Pages
- Sources for Convicts and Prisoners 1100-1986
  **www.catalogue.nationalarchives.gov.uk/
  RdLeaflet.asp?sLeafletID=253**

- Tracing 19th Century Criminals in the National Archives
  **www.catalogue.nationalarchives.gov.uk/
  RdLeaflet.asp?sLeafletID=120**

- Old Bailey and the Central Criminal Court: Criminal Trials
  **www.catalogue.nationalarchives.gov.uk/
  RdLeaflet.asp?sLeafletID=172**

- Assizes: Criminal Trials
  **www.catalogue.nationalarchives.gov.uk/
  RdLeaflet.asp?sLeafletID=154**

- Supreme Court: Appeal Cases after 1875
  **www.catalogue.nationalarchives.gov.uk/
  RdLeaflet.asp?sLeafletID=187**

- Supreme Court, Chancery Division: Cases after 1875
  **www.catalogue.nationalarchives.gov.uk/
  RdLeaflet.asp?sLeafletID=173**

- King's Bench (Crown Side) 1675-1875
  **www.catalogue.nationalarchives.gov.uk/
  RdLeaflet.asp?sLeafletID=177**

- Chancery Proceedings: Equity Suits from 1558
  **www.catalogue.nationalarchives.gov.uk/
  RdLeaflet.asp?sLeafletID=165**

- Equity Proceedings in the Court of Exchequer
  **www.catalogue.nationalarchives.gov.uk/
  RdLeaflet.asp?sLeafletID=160**

- Coroners' Inquests
  **www.catalogue.nationalarchives.gov.uk/
  RdLeaflet.asp?sLeafletID=175**

Further Reading
- HAWKINGS, DAVID T. *Criminal ancestors: a guide to historical criminal records in England and Wales.* Stroud: Sutton Publishing, 1992.

Quarter Sessions
- GIBSON, J.S.W. *Quarter sessions records for family historians: a select list.* 4th ed. F.F.H.S., 1995.
- McLAUGHLIN, EVE. *Quarter sessions: your ancestor and the law.* Haddenham: Varneys Press, 1995.
- EMMISON, F.G., & GRAY, IRVINE. *County records (Quarter sessions, petty sessions, clerk of the peace, and lieutenancy).* [Rev. ed.] Help for students of history **62.** Historical Association, 1987.

Civil Litigation

- HORWITZ, HENRY. *Exchequer equity records and proceedings 1649-1841.* Public Record Office handbook **32**. 2001.

Coroners' Records

- GIBSON, JEREMY, & ROGERS, COLIN. *Coroners' records in England and Wales.* 2nd ed. F.F.H.S., 2000.
- BARNARD, SYLVIA M. *Viewing the breathless corpse: coroners and inquests in Victorian Leeds.* Leeds. Words & Woodmere, 2001.

Chapter 18

Parliamentary Papers

This book has repeatedly stressed that the nineteenth century was an age of reform, and that those reforms led to the production of sources which are vital for the genealogist. Reform of the franchise, of the poor law, of probate, the introduction of civil registration, the compilation of the census - all these had important consequences for record keeping, and for the availability of the information upon which we now rely. The history of those reforms can largely be read in the pages of the Parliamentary papers.

Few people appreciate just how much information was crammed into these papers in the nineteenth century. They were undoubtedly the major publishing project of the period (as they continue to be into the twenty-first century). The reports of royal commissions, select committees, committees of inquiry, and inspectors, annual reports and other papers of governmental organizations, white papers, *etc., etc.*, were all included in the serried ranks of 'blue books' (as they were called) which still fill the basements of many libraries. Fortunately, they are now also available on microfiche.

Genealogists rarely consult these papers, although there is much information in them worthy of their attention. For example, the first listing of the nonconformist registers now in the custody of the National Archives was published by the commission which collected them. Their list has been superseded, but it does include the names of all the nonconformist ministers of the churches which sent registers in (1837-38, XXVIII, 377). There are a variety of other lists of names. The most well-known of these to genealogists is probably the *Return of owners of land, 1873,* (1874, LXXII) which has in recent years been reprinted in separate county sections by various publishers, and is also available on CD. Less well known, but perhaps of even more use to the genealogist, is the listing of 14,216 paupers in the return of the "name of every adult pauper in each workhouse who has been an inmate of the Workhouse during a continuous period of five years". (1861, LV, 201). Fifteen of these had been inmates for over sixty years!

Another return lists the *Destitute poor removed from England and Scotland to Ireland* in 1861 and 1862 (1863, LII, 267), and in 1863 (1864, LII, 305). Quite a number of returns deal with particular removals under the settlement laws; for example, Margaret McCarthy's removal from Lambeth to Ireland caused several letters to pass between the guardians of both workhouses and the Poor Law Board, which can be found at 1851 XLIX.163. Many reports deal with the state of particular workhouses, and with a wide variety of other poor law matters.

The poor law is extremely well documented in the Parliamentary papers, but the range of subjects treated is far wider than this. The Paris Exhibition of 1867, for example, was reported on by the *return of the names of all persons employed or engaged by the Department of Science and Art,* (1867-68, LV, 349) which specifies the duties, the previous employment, and the remuneration of the staff sent to Paris by the Department. On the same microfiche can be found the *Return of the number of certificates of naturalization issued to aliens* for 1854 to 1868 (1867-68, LV, 361), which gives names, places of birth, and dates of naturalization, and is the first return in a series which continues into the twentieth century.

Nominal returns are perhaps the most useful papers for genealogists. However, there is also much of interest to be found in the reports of royal commissions and select committees, *etc.* These bodies frequently questioned numerous witnesses at length concerning, for example, conditions in agriculture or mining, labour relations or local government. Their answers were taken down verbatim and printed in full. For example, the fourth report of the Royal Commission on Agricultural Depression (1896, xvii, 1) includes extensive evidence from seventy witnesses.

Unfortunately, the means for identifying particular papers likely to contain information of genealogical interest are not very good. There are many guides, but they are not designed for genealogical purposes. In order to use them, you need to use their indexes, and to understand the way in which the papers are arranged. This can be complex, since a variety of numbering systems are used. However, the probability here is that you will need to consult the microfiche edition. If so, they are bound up according to the parliamentary session, and each volume is given a volume number (usually quoted in Roman numerals). This may be followed by a page number; this refers to the number written by hand on each page, rather than to the page numbering of individual papers (many of which may be included in one volume). Hence 1896, xvii, 1, refers to volume 17 of the 1896 session, from the first page. A number of different indexes are available; however, Cockton is now authoritative. The Bopcris web-site lists c.5,000 key documents of the nineteenth century, and will in time digitise them. Powell provides a useful briefer guide for local historians, which may also be of some value to family historians.

Web Page
- Printed Parliamentary papers
  www.catalogue.nationalarchives.gov.uk/
  RdLeaflet.asp?sLeafletID=81

- Bopcris: unlocking key British Government Publications
  www.bopcris.ac.uk

Further Reading

- COCKTON, PETER. *Subject catalogue of the House of Commons Parliamentary papers 1801-1900.* 5 vols. Chadwyck-Healey, 1988.
- POWELL, W.R. *Local history from blue books: a select list of the sessional papers of the House of Commons.* Helps for students of history **64.** Historical Association, 1969.

Chapter 19

Migration

England has always been both a source of emigrants and a destination for immigrants. It has also been a transit station for Europeans emigrating to the new world. It has been estimated that no less than 9,000,000 emigrants passed through Liverpool alone on their way to a new life in North America. The convicts who sailed to Australia were fewer in number, but nevertheless their numbers were significant, as were the emigrants who sailed to South Africa and New Zealand. In the nineteenth century, the British Empire was at almost its fullest extent, and many British administrators and soldiers went to govern the colonies - especially India.

There were far fewer immigrants. The Irish were probably the most noticeable; they flooded into England during the years of the great famine in the 1840's, as well as taking passage to North America; many also crossed the Irish Sea for seasonal work, as they had done for centuries, and as they continued to do into the twentieth century. Their names are common in English records, especially those of the poor law and the census.

Others came as political or religious refugees: French clergy and aristocracy fleeing the revolution,

Jews seeking refuge from persecution in Tsarist eastern Europe, Italian and German revolutionaries (such as Marx) hiding themselves in the British Museum library. Others came for economic reasons: many German clerical workers sought to take advantage of greater opportunities in London than existed at home.

Records of migrants should be sought in both their countries of origin, and in the countries where they settled. Baxter provides useful guidance on the records of European countries which sent migrants to England. There are a wide variety of guides to tracing family history in the countries where English migrants settled, a select few of which are listed below.

The standard guides to English migration records are provided by Kershaw's two books. The rest of this chapter is essentially a summary of the information provided in them, although it should be noted that they are primarily devoted to records held by the National Archives and pay less attention to archives held in other local and national record offices.

Birth marriage and death registers are, as has already been noted, one of the first sources that should be consulted by genealogists. In order to trace emigrants, it may be necessary to consult registers kept by the appropriate authorities in countries of settlement. However, registers were maintained by British consuls, expatriate churches, and British forces stationed overseas; many have been deposited in

London repositories. Only a brief summary of these can be given here; they are listed by Yeo, and Kershaw's *Emigrants ...* may also be consulted. The Family Records Centre holds consular registers from 1849, marine registers of events at sea from 1837, and various registers of overseas forces. These are fully indexed, but cannot be directly consulted; application must be made for a certificate. The National Archives also holds the indexes to these registers, together with many of the original sources from which the General Register Office constructed its registers. Consular returns, together with a variety of other registers, are in RG 32-6, indexed in RG 43; some, but not all, of these duplicate material in the Family Records Centre. The deaths of seamen, 1851-90 are registered in BT 153 and indexed in BT 154-5. Passenger births, marriages, and deaths, 1854-83, are recorded in BT 158, which also includes births and deaths 1883-7, and deaths 1888-90. A small number of regimental registers are held amongst War Office records. There are also three registers relating to emigrants at sea in CO 386/170-72. Bevan's *Tracing your ancestors in the Public Record Office,* section 4.14-15, provides details of registers and indexes available in the National Archives.

The episcopal oversight of Anglican churches and chaplains overseas was the responsibility of the Bishop of London. He therefore, received many original registers and bishops' transcripts, especially from European churches, but also for many congregations on other continents. These are lodged in the Guildhall Library, and listed by Yeo. He also lists many Anglican registers returned to the Archbishop of Canterbury, and held at Lambeth Palace Library.

The British Library's India Office Records holds over 1,100 registers relating to areas formerly administered by the East India Company. These are described on its web-site and relate not only to the Indian sub-continent (including the areas now known as Burma and Pakistan), but also to places such as Kuwait, Aden, St. Helena, *etc.* The Library also holds many transcripts of monumental inscriptions. The British Association for Cemeteries in South Asia (**www.ozemail.com.au/~clday/bacsa.htm**) has a particular interest in this area, and may be worth contacting.

If it is necessary to have recourse to records held in countries of settlement, then it should be noted that the *International genealogical index,* discussed in chapter 4 above, indexes innumerable colonial and foreign registers. Furthermore, copies of the sources it indexes can be obtained on microfilm through any Latter Day Saints Family History Centre (see chapter 1). Many transcripts of overseas registers, both printed and manuscript, are held by the Society of Genealogists.

Passenger lists are another important source. They were compiled for most sailings, and many survive - although only a small proportion of the lists actually compiled. Filby and Meyer have indexed over 3,000,000 entries in published lists of passengers to North America (not all of these were nineteenth-century). A rapidly increasing number of passenger lists are being transcribed for the internet; some of the more important web-sites are listed below.

Most passenger lists held in the National Archives post-date 1876. There are exceptions to this rule: FO 83/21-2 contains lists of aliens arriving in Britain in 1810-11; there is an index to aliens certificates of arrival 1826-49 in HO 5/25-32; the original certificates for 1836-52 are in HO 2; HO 3 includes lists of alien passengers 1836-60 and 1867-9; passenger lists for Mediterranean steam packets, 1831-4 are in ADM 30/35. The Anglo-German Family History Society (**www.art-science.com/agfhs**) has indexed some of these sources.

The most important archive of passenger lists in the National Archives are those collected by the Board of Trade from 1878. They are filed in two series, arrivals (BT 26) and departures (BT 27). In nineteenth century lists, the information given is usually name, age and occupation. BT 26 only includes lists from ships which arrived from ports outside of Europe or the Mediterranean (although they may have called at European ports to pick up passengers). Most, but not all, pre-1890 arrival lists were destroyed. Unfortunately, the lists in BT 26 and BT 27 are not indexed. In order to locate a particular entry, you need to know the month and the port of arrival or departure.

Many passenger lists are held in the archives of countries of settlement. From 1820, ships' captains arriving in the U.S.A. were required to file them with the collector of customs at the port of arrival. The information given usually includes place of origin, date of arrival, destination in the U.S.A., occupation, age and gender. Some ninety per cent of these lists have survived; many have been indexed, and microfilms are widely available in the United States. Details are given on the U.S. National Archives and Records Administration website.

Even more information is given on the U.S. Immigration Passenger Lists, which commence after 1891, and supersede the Customs lists. These include marital status, occupation, last residence, and, if joining a relative, the relative's name, address and relationship. Some of these lists have also been indexed; the Ellis Island project has indexed no less than 22,000,000 names of passengers who arrived in New York between 1892 and 1924; its database is on the internet at **www.ellisisland.org**

Some passenger lists are also available in Australia, Canada, New Zealand and South Africa. There are many websites devoted to these; the more important one are listed below. Kershaw's *Emigrants ...* also provides some detailed information.

Passport records provide another potential source of information, although passports were not as widely used in the nineteenth century as they are today; they tended to be confined to diplomats and merchants, and were not compulsory for overseas travel. Registers of passports, 1794-1948, are held in the National Archives (FO 610); these note applicants' names and destinations. Indexes of passport applicants for 1851-62 and 1874-1916 are in FO 611; these are now available online (see below).

More nineteenth-century migrants are recorded in passenger lists than in any other single source, with the possible exception of birth, marriage and death registers. However, neither lists nor registers are capable of providing comprehensive coverage of migrants, passport records even less so. Fortunately, there are a multitude of other potential sources of information both in the National Archives, and in the archives of the countries where emigrants settled. The former are discussed in detail in Kershaw's two books; he also gives many pointers towards the latter.

There were many different reasons for emigration, and also for temporary residence overseas. Civil servants and army officers were sent to govern the colonies, or to represent the United Kingdom in other countries. The newly formed Poor Law unions exported their paupers to Australia, Canada, or anywhere else they could. Those who narrowly escaped the clutches of the workhouse often decided that they would be better off in North America, or, perhaps, Australia. If they were unfortunate enough to be caught stealing a loaf of bread, the courts might decide for them that they would be better off in New South Wales. Charities such as Dr. Barnardo's decided that many of the children they cared for would also be better off in the colonies. All of these groups, and others, left records of their activities, in which can be traced the comings and goings of our ancestors.

The careers of colonial administrators and diplomats can be traced in the *British imperial calendar,* published annually from 1810, the *Foreign Office list,* from 1852, and the *Colonial Office list,* from 1862. All these are available in major reference libraries. Senior civil servants are likely to be mentioned in the many biographical dictionaries in the *British biographical archive,* or in the *Dictionary of national biography.*

India played a particularly important role in the history of England during the eighteenth and nineteenth centuries; many middle and upper class families sent members to serve the Company or the Crown. Until 1858, the sub-continent was administered by the East India Company; thereafter its government was directly controlled by the India Office. The careers of administrators and soldiers can be traced in outline by consulting the *East India register,* published from 1803 to 1858, and its successor, the *Indian Army and Civil Service list;* runs are sometimes held in major reference libraries, as well as in the British Library. The records of both the Company and the India Office are held in the latter's Oriental and India Office collections; they are listed by Moir; biographical sources are described by Baxter. Numerous other useful publications, including a variety of name lists, are itemised in Raymond's *Occupational sources for genealogists* (2nd ed; F.F.H.S., 1996).

Reference has already been made to the British Library's holdings of Indian birth, marriage and death registers. Also available are writers petitions (i.e. job applications), which include educational and baptismal details, service records for both army and civil officers, probate records, *etc.* The archives of Haileybury College, which was established by the Company in 1806 to train its servants, are particularly important. The library has compiled a biographical index to many of these records (including the registers); there are almost 300,000 entries.

East India Company servants came from the opposite end of the social spectrum to the poor who were exported by overseers and boards of guardians. Parish and union records (chapter 11) may record the latter; names may be mentioned in overseers accounts or vestry minutes, or lists may have been drawn up separately. Lists may also have been sent to the Poor Law Commissioners in London, and may now be found in the National Archives (MH 12). Unfortunately, MH 12 has no subject listing; it also includes much other correspondence, and is arranged chronologically by county and union. Its voluminousness renders it difficult to use for genealogical purposes.

In addition to the poor law authorities, a number of

charities were also involved in arranging emigration of poor and orphaned children. Dr. Barnardo's was one of the best known of these organizations, but there were many others. The web-page on child emigration listed below identifies many of those involved. The Social Work Archives of the University of Liverpool **sca.lib.liv.ac.uk/collections/socialwork/home.htm** describes the archives of Dr. Barnardo's, and of several other sending agencies.

Assistance with emigration was also available from the Land and Emigration Commission, established in 1833 to promote emigration by offering free passage and making land grants; its records are in the National Archives. Amongst them are its emigration entry books 1814-71 (CO 385) and its papers (CO 386) which identify names. The Colonial Office's emigration original correspondence (CO 384) includes many letters from emigrants in North America, the West Indies, and Australia.

Emigration to Australia began with convicts. Much information on transportation has been published; Vine-Hall's bibliography provides details. The Australian Joint Copying Project has microfilmed many English records relating to transportation, and its handbooks provide useful lists, whether you are consulting the microfilm in Australia, or the original sources in various English record offices.

One of the best sources of personal information on convicts are the pleas for clemency to be found in the National Archives criminal petitions (HO 17 & HO 18);

these frequently include details of family background and personal circumstances. The original trial records are more formal and less informative; assize and quarter sessions records are discussed in chapter 17.

In addition to the records of emigration and immigration found in British archives, much is to be found in the repositories of countries where emigrants settled. These cannot be discussed in detail here; the researcher should consult a guide to the records of the particular country concerned. A number of such guides are listed below.

Web Pages
Immigrants
- Immigrants
  www.catalogue.nationalarchives.gov.uk/
                    RdLeaflet.asp?sLeafletID=243

- Moving Here
  www.movinghere.org.uk/

Emigrants
- Emigrants
  www.catalogue.nationalarchives.gov.uk/
                    rdleaflet.asp?sLeafletID=292

- Emigration
  www.familyrecords.gov.uk/topics/
                    emigration__2.htm

- The Registers of Names of Passport Applications 1851 to 1862 and 1874 to 1903
  www.nationalarchivist.com/index04/about.cfm
  Database; pay per view site.

- Passenger Lists
  www.catalogue.nationalarchives.gov.uk/ RdLeaflet.asp?sLeafletID=106

- Immigrant Ships Transcribers Guild
  www.immigrantships.net/

- Ship's Passenger Lists: Hugh Reekie's Index of Indexes
  members.allstream.net/~max-com/Ships.html

Australia
- Australian Family History Compendium
  www.cohsoft.com.au/afhc/

- Transportation to Australia 1787-1868
  www.catalogue.nationalarchives.gov.uk/ rdLeaflet.asp?sLeafletID=347

- Australian Joint Copying Project
  www.nla.gov.au/collect/ajcp.html

Canada
- Cyndis List: Canada - General
  www.cyndislist.com/gencam.htm

India

- British Library India Office Records
  www.bl.uk/collections/orientaloffice.html

New Zealand

- New Zealand Society of Genealogists
  www.genealogy.org.nz

- Migration [Archives New Zealand]
  www.archives.govt.nz/docs/pdfs/
  Ref_Guide_Migration.pdf

South Africa

- South African Genealogy
  home.global.co.za/~mercon/

- Heather's South African Genealogy Help List
  www.genealogy.co.za/

- British 1820 Settlers to South Africa
  www.1820settlers.com/index.php

United States

- Cyndis List
  www.Cyndislist.com

- Emigrants to North America after 1776
  www.catalogue.nationalarchives.gov.uk/
  RdLeaflet.asp?sLeafletID=106

- Notes for Americans on Tracing their British
  Ancestry
  www.sog.org.uk/Leaflets/americans.html

- NARA [National Archives & Records Administration]:
  Genealogy
  www.archives.gov/research_room/genealogy/

- Ellis Island Foundation, Inc.
  www.ellisisland.org/
  Passenger arrival records

Further Reading
Immigration
- BAXTER, A. *In search of your European roots: a
  complete guide to tracing your ancestors in every
  country in Europe.* 3rd ed. Genealogical Publishing
  Co., 2001.
- KERSHAW, ROGER, & PEARSALL, MARK. *Immigrants
  and aliens: a guide to sources on U.K. immigration
  and citizenship.* Research guide, **25.** National
  Archives, 2004.

Emigration
- KERSHAW, ROGER. *Emigrants and expats: a guide to
  sources on U.K. emigration and residents overseas.*
  Public Record Office readers guide **20.** 2002.
- YEO, GEOFFREY. *The British overseas: a guide to
  records of their baptisms, births, marriages, deaths
  and burials available in the United Kingdom.* 3rd ed.
  Guildhall Library, 1994.

- WATTS, CHRISTOPHER, & WATTS, MICHAEL. *Tracing births, deaths and marriages at sea.* Society of Genealogists, 2004.

Australia

- VINE HALL, NICK. *Tracing your family history in Australia: a guide to sources.* 3rd ed. Albert Park: N. Vine Hall, 2002.
- VINE HALL, NICK. *Tracing your family history in Australia: a bibliography.* Mt. Eliza: N. Vine Hall, 2002.
- SHEEHAN, C. *The Australian Joint Copying Project for family historians.* Brisbane. Library Board of Queensland, 1987.

Canada

- BAXTER, ANGUS. *In search of your Canadian roots: tracing your family tree in Canada.* 3rd ed. Baltimore: Genealogical Publishing, 2000.

India

- BAXTER, I.A. *India Office Library and records: a brief guide to biographical sources.* 2nd ed. India Office Library & Records (British Library), 1990.
- MOIR, M. *A general guide to the India Office records.* British Library, 1988.

New Zealand

- BROMELL, ANNE. *Tracing family history in New Zealand.* Godwit, 1996.

- KALOPULU, KAREN, & DEANNE, ROSEMARY. *Researching family history in the collections of Auckland City Libraries.* 5th ed. Auckland Public Library, 1997.

South Africa
- LOMBARD, R.T. *Handbook for genealogical research in South Africa.* 3rd ed. Pretoria: H.S.R.C., 1990.

United States
- EAKLE, A., & CERNY, J. *The source: a guide book of American genealogy,* ed. Loretto Dennis Szucs, & Sandra Hargreaves Luebking. Rev. ed. Salt Lake City: Ancestry Publishing, 1996.
- FILBY, P.W., & MEYER, M.K. *Passenger and immigration lists index: a guide to published arrival records of about 500,000 passengers who came to the United States and Canada in the 17th, 18th and 19th centuries.* 3 vols. Detroit: Gale, 1981. Continued by annual supplements. The works indexed are listed in: FILBY, P.W. *Passenger and immigration lists bibliography 1538-1900, being a guide to published lists of arrivals in the United States and Canada.* 2nd ed. Detroit: Gale, 1988.

Appendix 1

Addresses

Some addresses of institutions have been given in the body of the text above. Those which have been mentioned repeatedly, or are generally important, are listed here.

Society of Genealogists
14 Charterhouse Buildings
London
EC1M 7BA

www.sog.org.uk

Federation of Family History Societies
P.O.Box 2425
Coventry CV5 6XX

www.ffhs.org.uk

Guild of One Name Studies
Box G,
14, Charterhouse Buildings,
Goswell Road
London, EC1M 7BA

www.one-name.org/intro.html

National Archives
Ruskin Avenue
Kew, Richmond
Surrey, TW9 4DU

www.nationalarchives.gov.uk

Family Records Centre
1 Myddleton Street
London, EC1R 1UW

www.familyrecords.gov.uk/frc/default.htm

British Library
96 Euston Road
London, NW1 2DB

www.bl.uk

Guildhall Library
Aldermanbury
London, EC2

www.ihrinfo.ac.uk/gh

Index

204